SPECIALTY DIVER
DEEP DIVING

SSI®
SCUBA SCHOOLS INTERNATIONAL

DISCLAIMER:

The information contained in the SSI training materials is intended to give an individual enrolled in a training course a broad perspective of the diving activity. There are many recommendations and suggestions regarding the use of standard and specialized equipment for the activity. Not all of the equipment discussed in the training material can, or will, be used in this activity. The choice of equipment and techniques used in the course is determined by the location of the activity, the environmental conditions and other factors.

A choice of equipment and techniques cannot be made until the dive site is surveyed immediately prior to the dive. Based on the dive site, the decision should be made regarding which equipment and techniques shall be used. The decision is that of the dive leader *and* the individual enrolled in the training course.

The intent of all SSI training materials is to give individuals as much information as possible in order for individuals to make their own decisions regarding the diving activity, what equipment should be used and what specific techniques may be needed. The ultimate decision on when and how to dive is that of the individual diver.

Copyright © 1991 by Concept Systems, Inc.

ISBN: 1-880229-04-8

First Edition
    First Printing, 12/91
    Second Printing, 2/93

Second Edition
    First Printing, 6/96

Printed in the USA.

SCUBA SCHOOLS INTERNATIONAL
2619 Canton Court • Fort Collins, Co 80525-4498
(970) 482-0883 • Fax (970) 482-6157
e-mail: admin@ssiusa.com

CONTENTS

REORDER #2501DD

ACKNOWLEDGMENTS

Editor in Chief	**Laurie K. Humpal**
Co-Authors	**Hal Watts** **Laurie K. Humpal**
Art Director	**David M. Pratt**
Graphic Designer	**Betsy Musso**
Photographers	**Greg Ochocki** **Blake Miller**
Technical Editors	**Robert Clark** **Gary Clark** **Ed Christini** **Katherine Ferretti** **Dave Haddad** **Curt Wiessner** **Tom Wilk** **Roy Williams**
Proofing Editor	**Linda J. Clark**

Special Thanks To:
Joe Ault • Kie McCarthy • Elton Moore

FOREWORD

WHY SPECIALTY TRAINING? The answer to "why specialty training?" is quite simple. An entry level course provides you with the motor skills, equipment knowledge, and minimum open water experience needed to be considered a safe diver. However, an Open Water Diver Course does not a specialist make.

Specialty training has two primary objectives: to prepare you for new diving situations, and to improve your level of skill. The SSI Specialty Diver Program provides an excellent introduction to a variety of different diving subjects such as Deep Diving, Boat Diving, Night Diving/Limited Visibility, and many others. These courses are designed to enhance both the enjoyment and comfort of each new situation. Specialty training also develops your current level of skill to a much higher level. For example, you may have learned how to follow a compass in your entry level course—SSI's Navigation Specialty course can teach you how to navigate! A specialty course takes you clearly beyond what you may have learned in your Open Water Diver Course.

Each specialty generates its own excitement and opens its own doors. Not every specialty is appropriate to every diver or diving level. Some specialties may not be available in your area, but can be enjoyed when traveling. Every specialty, however, can open new vistas for the diver who wishes to explore all the adventures scuba diving can provide!

The SSI Specialty Diver Program offers the opportunity, through continuing education, to accelerate the learning process that otherwise could only be gained through significant, time-consuming experience. You can quickly prepare yourself to be comfortable in whatever diving situations apply to you personally. Here is a simple, inexpensive way to gain knowledge, experience, safety and recognition, in classes tailored to your specific interests!

THE SSI SPECIALTY DIVER PROGRAM OFFERS THE OPPORTUNITY TO ACCELERATE THE LEARNING PROCESS THAT COULD OTHERWISE BE GAINED ONLY THROUGH TIME-CONSUMING EXPERIENCE.

DEEP DIVE
PLANNING

1

CHAPTER 1:
DEEP DIVE PLANNING

Often the question is asked: "Why dive deep?" Deep diving opens the door to many new and exciting dive sites. These sites include deeper wrecks, reefs, wall dives, and more (Figure 1-1—see page 2). People participate in deep diving for various reasons. However, most divers are interested in enhancing and improving their skill and confidence level while taking the deep diver course. Curiosity is ever present in humans. Most divers feel the need to explore and wonder what lies "beyond"— even if we do not have the desire to look for ourselves. How many of us, while wall diving at 60 feet (18 metres) have not wondered what spectacular sites and hidden beauty lie below? Probably no one.

But Deep Diving training does more for Open Water Divers than satisfy curiosity. Those who have graduated from a deep diving course have found that their diving skills have greatly improved, especially their

buoyancy control and breathing rate. They have also reported that their mental awareness of depth, direction, environment, remaining air and the buddy system have improved.

During this course, you will learn how to plan and execute a deep dive with a higher degree of comfort, by obtaining a better understanding of the factors involved in deep diving. Let us begin by taking a look at the deep diving limits, how deep diving differs from other types of specialty diving, and the importance of planning to the deep diving process.

Figure 1-1 *Deep diving opens the door to many new and exciting dive sites.*

DEEP DIVING LIMITS

When we talk about deep diving, we must realize that depth is a relative term. What may be shallow in some diving conditions, may be deep under other conditions, such as cold, murky or fast moving waters. In the clear, warm waters of the Florida springs, as well as the Caribbean and South Pacific, a diver will be much more comfortable deep diving than in the colder, darker waters found on the northern coastlines of the Atlantic and Pacific oceans. Your deep diving limits are based not only on the environment, but also on your personal experience level, comfort level, and skill level. What may be a deep dive to you may be shallow to another diver, which is fine, for as in all types of diving, each diver must set his or her own personal diving limits.

Because many people enjoy pushing their own personal limits, the recreational diving industry has established deep diving limits that they recommend recreational divers adhere to. These limits are not arbitrary, but are based on Doppler ultrasound research, and have been established for the safety of the diving community.

> DEPTH IS A RELATIVE TERM: WHAT IS CONSIDERED SHALLOW IN SOME DIVING CONDITIONS MAY BE DEEP UNDER OTHER CONDITIONS.

0-60 Feet (0-18 Metres)

When you began diving in your Open Water Diver class, you began in the shallow end of the pool, and may have eventually progressed to water as deep as 60 feet (18 metres) in your final open water training. At this point in your diving career, you were still not sure about your equipment, controlling your buoyancy, and the other new skills you had learned in your course. The entry-level training limit is set at 60 feet for a good reason, because anything over that is considered "deep diving."

As you began to log dives, however, you started to feel more comfortable with your skills and started to think that it might be nice to explore beyond the 60 foot depth limit.

60-100 Feet (18-30 Metres)

You learned in your entry-level course that after Open Water Diver certification the recommended limit for recreational diving is 100 feet (30 metres), due to the increased effects of the partial pressure of nitrogen on the human body at depth. These effects, such as nitrogen narcosis and decompression sickness, will be discussed in further detail in Chapter 4. The safety considerations for deep diving go beyond the effects of nitrogen, for deep diving is an activity that requires physical and mental preparedness. When divers put 100 feet of water between themselves and the surface, they must have the physical and mental skill level required for the situation, as well as more sophisticated diving equipment.

This skill level is usually acquired by logging dives under the supervision of a dive leader or with a properly trained and more experienced dive buddy.

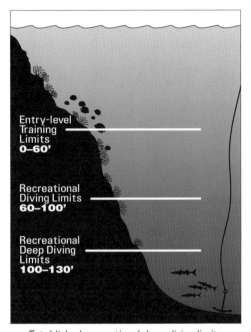

Established recreational deep diving limits.

100-130 Feet (30-39 Metres)

The 100 to 130 foot depth limits are recommended only for those divers that are experienced and qualified. When a diver ventures below the 100 foot recreational limit, he begins a whole new level of diving. The effects of pressure multiply when using air at these depths, increasing the risk. Bottom time is drastically reduced, requiring careful planning and monitoring. There is less room for error at these greater depths, and only qualified divers truly understand the extra preparation and skill that is required to dive to the 130 foot (39 metre) limit.

As mentioned earlier, the maximum limit of 130 feet is not an arbitrary number; it was derived through Doppler ultrasound research. By looking at the Doppler limits on the U.S. Navy tables, you can see that you can stay at 130 feet for 5 minutes, but beyond that, you have exceeded the Doppler limits and are subjecting yourself to increased risk for decompression sickness.

Because the U.S. Navy tables were developed for Navy divers, and not for the average recreational diver of today, the Doppler limits were established to help increase the safety factor. Doppler research will be discussed later in Chapter 4 under Decompression Sickness.

> **N O T E :**   *THERE IS NO GUARANTEE THAT STAYING WITHIN THESE LIMITS WILL INSURE SAFETY. EVERY DIVER IS DIFFERENT, AND INDIVIDUAL NITROGEN ABSORPTION RATES WILL VARY TO SOME DEGREE. RESPONSIBLE DIVERS PLAN THEIR DIVES THOROUGHLY, AND PART OF THIS PLANNING IS USING THE DOPPLER LIMITS AND STAYING CONSERVATIVELY WITHIN THEM. MONITORING YOUR ASCENT RATE, AND THE INCLUSION OF A 3 TO 5 MINUTE STOP AT 15 FEET (5 METRES) ADDS A MARGIN OF SAFETY.*

Now that we have introduced the deep diving limits and why it is important to dive within them, let us go on and look at the importance of planning to deep diving.

DEEP DIVE PLANNING

Dive planning is an important part of any dive, but it becomes even more essential when diving deep. Up to this point in your diving career, you may, or may not, have been using strict dive planning. If you tend to dive shallow, or with a leader or more experienced diver, you may have either skipped the planning stage or left it up to your buddy. When deep diving, each person is an important part of the plan, and should participate in the planning process (Figure 1-2). The process provides each team member a chance to make sure the dive will fit their own objective, skill and comfort level. This way, you will not be getting involved with a dive

Figure 1-2   *When deep diving, each person is an important part of the plan and should participate in the planning process.*

beyond your comfort zone. A well planned dive is safer, and besides, the planning process is a fun, social exchange, which is one of the most enjoyable aspects of diving.

Objective

Each team member should understand and agree with the objective of the planned dive. The objective may be to explore a deep wreck, or to try to locate a reef, lobster or just anything of interest. If a buddy is not qualified for or interested in that objective, now is the time to make a new buddy team or change the objective.

Surface Consumption Rate & Minimum P.S.I.

The next step in deep diving planning is to figure your air consumption so you will know how much air you will use at a given depth. Your air consumption rate is affected by many factors that vary depending on your equipment, the conditions, and your comfort level. Some of the factors that affect your air consumption are listed below.

- *Physical size of diver*
- *Experience level of diver*
- *Fitness level of diver*
- *Stress level of diver*
- *Breathing habits of diver*
- *Work load performed on the dive*
- *Temperature of water*
- *Depth of the dive*
- *Breathing resistance from regulator*
- *Size of the tank*
- *Air loss due to leaks in tank valve, gauges or regulator*
- *Air required to equalize and maintain buoyancy with inflator*

Now that we have looked at what factors affect air consumption, the next step is to use a formula to figure what your actual rate is. We refer to this air consumption formula as Surface Consumption Rate (SCR). By knowing what your breathing rate is at the surface, you can calculate how long your tank of air will last at a certain depth. If you maintain a record of the air consumption rate for your dives, you can measure your comfort level, because the more comfortable you are, the less air you use.

Since the pressure gauge measures air pressure in pounds per square inch, PSI, you must know in advance how many psi per minute you will consume. Following is a simple formula you can use to determine your SCR. *Caution: Your SCR will change with tank size, so you will need to make a separate run with each different size tank you will use. The metric air consumption formula is in the appendix of this manual.*

SCR Formula:

$$\frac{(PSI \div \text{bottom time}) \times 33 \text{ feet*}}{\text{Depth} + 33 \text{ feet*}} = \begin{array}{l}\text{PSI consumed per minute at} \\ \text{surface, or at 1 atmosphere}\end{array}$$

Note: *In fresh water, use 34 feet in place of 33 feet for salt water.*

For the purposes of this formula, we will assume the following definitions:

PSI = Air consumed in a timed swim at a constant depth
Time = Duration of the timed swim in minutes
Depth = Depth of the timed swim in feet

Example: *A diver dives in salt water to 10 feet for 10 minutes and uses 300 PSI.*

$$\frac{(300 \div 10) \times (33)}{10 + 33} = 23 \text{ PSI per minute at the surface (SCR)}$$

Because the SCR expresses consumption at the surface, it must be converted to a rate consumed at depth to make it useful in dive planning. To demonstrate how much quicker your air is consumed at depth, let us use the SCR from the above example and show you what a diver at various depths (atmospheres) would consume:

Examples — Consumption Rates at Various Depths (Atmospheres):

2 Atmospheres: At 33 feet, a diver consumes air twice as fast as on the surface.

> **23 SCR x 2 ATM = 46 PSI consumed per minute at 33 feet.**

3 Atmospheres: At 66 feet, a diver consumes air three times as fast.

> **23 SCR x 3 ATM = 69 PSI consumed per minute at 66 feet.**

4 Atmospheres: At 99 feet, a diver consumes air four times as fast.

> **23 SCR x 4 ATM = 92 PSI consumed per minute at 99 feet.**

From the above example, a diver with a surface consumption rate (SCR) of 23 PSI per minute dives to 3 atmospheres, which increases the diver's consumption rate to 69 PSI per minute. The formula below shows how much time the diver would have at 66 feet with a 3000PSI tank. Because divers should surface with a minimum of 500 PSI in their tank, you should subtract that 500 pounds now and start your calculations with 2500 PSI.

Example:
- Diver with an SCR of 23 PSI/minute
- Dives to 3 atmospheres, increasing the SCR to 69 PSI/minute.
- Diver has a 3000PSI tank (only count 2500PSI)
- How much time does the diver have at 66 feet?

> **(2500 PSI) ÷ (69 PSI/minute) = 36 minutes at 66 feet**

Should you want to calculate your air consumption for an exact depth such as 110 feet, and you know your SCR is 23, simply divide your SCR by 1 atmosphere to determine your consumption rate per foot. By multiplying your depth (110 feet) by your consumption per foot (.7 PSI), then adding your SCR (23 PSI), you arrive at your consumption rate for an exact depth. See the formula below for a better explanation.

Example:

Step 1: *23 PSI (your SCR) ÷ 33 feet = .7 PSI (consumption/ft.)*

Step 2: *.7 PSI x 110 feet = 77 PSI + 23 PSI (SCR) = 100 PSI/minute at 110 feet.*

NOTE: The metric air consumption calculations are in the appendix of this manual.

When planning a deep dive, you should buddy up with a diver who has an SCR similar to yours and who is using the same volume tank (Figure 1-3). If you do not know your SCR, your SSI Instructor can help you calculate it.

Running out of air at depth is extremely dangerous and completely avoidable. An out-of-air situation can result if divers do not realize that their air is used up more

Figure 1-3 *When planning a deep dive, you should buddy up with a diver who has an SCR similar to yours and who is using the same volume tank.*

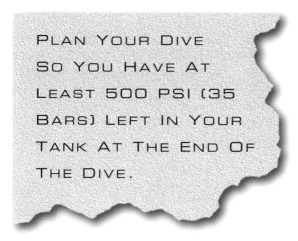

PLAN YOUR DIVE SO YOU HAVE AT LEAST 500 PSI (35 BARS) LEFT IN YOUR TANK AT THE END OF THE DIVE.

quickly at increased depths, or if they fail to keep a constant check of both their own and their buddy's pressure gauge. This is why you must plan your deep dive so you have a minimum of 500 PSI (35 bars) left in your tank at the end of the dive.

Maximum Depth and Bottom Time

The next step in deep dive planning is to determine a maximum depth and bottom time for the dive. The deeper you dive the less time (leeway) you have in planning. Therefore, it leaves no room for chance. For example, if your planned depth is 120 feet (36 metres), you have a no-decompression bottom time limit of 10 minutes. If after 5 minutes you accidentally drop down to 130 feet (39 metres), you have already maximized your bottom time and will need to ascend.

To refresh your memory, the definition of *depth* is the deepest point you reached during your dive, even if it was only momentarily. When we speak of *bottom time*, we are referring to the elapsed time, starting from when you begin your descent, until the time you begin a direct ascent to the surface.

If you do not have a diving computer, you should always take the dive tables with you under water so you can replan your dive if needed. However, since this may be impractical at times, it is best to pre-plan your dive for more flexibility by creating contingency plans to various depths. For example, you may want to dive between 90 and 120 feet (27-36 metres) depending on what you see under water. You can prepare your contingency plans on a slate by writing both the no-decompression bottom time limit and your air consumption limit for each depth. This is because your air consumption may be more limiting than your bottom time, and you will not want to stay down longer than your air supply will last. Remember, your 500 PSI (35 bars) reserve should be subtracted out of your air consumption limit so it will be there for emergencies.

Example (Calculations based on an SCR of 23):

Maximum Depth	Doppler Limit	Air Limit
90 feet (25 metres)	25 minutes	28 minutes
100 feet (30 metres)	20 minutes	27 minutes
110 feet (33 metres)	15 minutes	25 minutes
120 feet (36 metres)	10 minutes	24 minutes

Remember, you will need to refigure this contingency plan for each repetitive dive because your bottom time limits will change throughout the diving day.

When planning a deep dive, be sure to limit the depth to the maximum that you and your buddy have been trained for. For example, a buddy team is planning a dive to 100 feet (30 metres); however, one of the buddies has never logged a dive over 60 feet (18 metres). The dive plan should be changed to a shallower depth. It should always be remembered that diving is a fun and social activity. This means that everyone should enjoy the dive and be comfortable. Part of planning is selecting parameters that meet the objective of the dive, but also meeting the comfort level of each member of the buddy team.

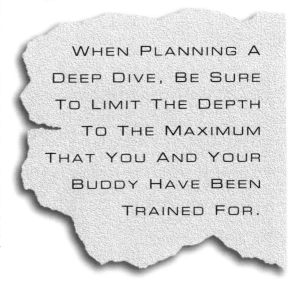

WHEN PLANNING A DEEP DIVE, BE SURE TO LIMIT THE DEPTH TO THE MAXIMUM THAT YOU AND YOUR BUDDY HAVE BEEN TRAINED FOR.

Environmental Conditions

The environmental conditions must be taken into consideration during the planning stages of any dive. These conditions may require changing the depth, bottom time or maybe even canceling the dive. Environmental conditions of concern would be: currents, visibility, surf and temperature.

Equipment

Deep diving requires higher quality and better maintained equipment than shallow diving. More information on deep diving equipment will be covered in the next chapter.

Communication

Communication between buddies is an important part of deep diving (Figure 1-4). You should be able to communicate any problems to your buddy, and he or she should be able to do the same. Hand signals should be gone over and agreed upon because many divers are taught or have picked up on different signals. So do not assume your buddy will understand your signals.

Figure 1-4   *Communication between buddies is an important part of deep diving.*

Important hand signals to agree on, to understand, and to use are:

☐ ok	☐ down	☐ watch me
☐ tired	☐ danger	☐ up
☐ look	☐ get neutral	☐ stop
☐ problem	☐ level off	
☐ show psi	☐ dizzy	

After diving with the same buddies for a while, you will most likely add or subtract hand signals. However, do not make underwater communications too hard to follow. The use of a slate is another way to communicate.

ALTITUDE AND DIVING

Because the dive tables were designed for use at sea level, when a diver flies in an aircraft or drives to altitude after diving, or actually dives at altitude, there is increased risk of decompression sickness. When planning a dive, you must understand the effects of altitude, and take your traveling plans into consideration.

Flying and Diving

When planning a deep dive, be sure to allow plenty of surface interval time before you plan on flying, especially after diving deep (Figure 1-5). Driving at high altitude also increases the risk of the bends after deep diving. SSI recommends that divers follow the DAN (Divers Alert Network) guidelines for going to altitude

Figure 1-5   *Be sure to allow plenty of surface interval time before you plan on flying, especially after diving deep.*

after diving. The guidelines listed below were established at a 1989 Undersea and Hyperbaric Medicine Society Workshop on flying after diving.

■ A **minimum surface interval of 12 hours** is required in order to be reasonably assured a diver will remain symptom free upon ascent to altitude in a commercial jet airliner (altitude up to 8000 feet or 2438 metres).
   Note: The Workshop participants did not discuss the risk of flying or driving to lower elevations, or the effect of dives at altitude. These guidelines therefore may be too conservative for these applications.

■ Divers who plan to make **daily, multiple dives for several days** or make dives that require decompression stops should take special precautions and wait for an extended surface interval beyond 12 hours before flight. The greater the duration before flight the less likely is decompression sickness to occur.

■ There can never be a flying after diving **rule** that is guaranteed to prevent decompression sickness completely. Rather, there can be a **guideline** that represents the best estimate for a conservative, safe surface interval for the vast majority of divers. There will always be an occasional diver whose physiological makeup or special diving circumstances will result in the bends.

■ Further research is recommended to provide significant data upon which to provide more specific guidelines for the future.

High Altitude Diving

High altitude diving requires using a special set of dive tables and/or a diving computer that takes into consideration the pressure at higher altitude, because the U.S. Navy tables were designed for diving at sea level (Figure 1-6). You should be aware that the models used to develop these tables are theoretical, and the no-decompression limits vary from table to table. Also, dive computers typically require time to adjust to the altitude before they work accurately. The best approach to diving at altitude is to dive conservatively. The higher you go, the more conservative you should be. If you are planning to do any high altitude diving, you should first contact a professional SSI dive store that is knowledgeable in this type of diving.

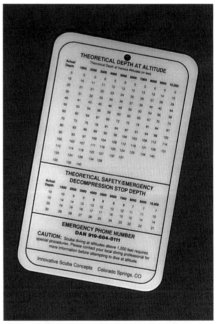

Figure 1-6 *High altitude diving requires using a special set of diving tables that take into consideration the pressure at higher altitude.*

As you can see by the amount of information covered in this chapter, deep dive planning is very important and extensive. During your deep diving experiences, you may come up with planning procedures other than those listed in this manual that are helpful and add to your diving pleasure and safety.

In Chapter 2 we will continue the planning process by looking at the equipment that is required for deep diving.

CHAPTER 1
REVIEW

1. Those who have graduated from a deep diving course have found their diving skills have greatly improved, especially their _____ control and _____ rate.

2. Your deep diving limits are based not only on the environment, but also on your personal _____ level, _____ level, and _____ level.

3. The 100 to 130 foot (30-39 metre) depth limits are recommended only for those divers who are _____ and _____.

4. The maximum limit of 130 feet (39 metres) is not an arbitrary number; it was derived through _____ _____ research.

5. By knowing what your breathing rate is at the surface, you can calculate how long your tank of air will last at a _____ _____.

6. When planning a deep dive, you should buddy up with a diver who has an _____ similar to yours and who is using the same volume tank.

7. When we speak of _____ _____ , we are referring to the elapsed time, starting from when you begin your descent, until the time you begin a direct ascent to the surface.

8. A minimum surface interval of _____ _____ is required in order to be reasonably assured a diver will remain symptom free upon ascent to altitude in a commercial jet airliner (altitude up to 8000 feet/2438 metres).

9. High altitude diving requires using a special set of _____ _____ and/or a diving computer that takes into consideration the pressure at higher altitude.

DEEP DIVING
EQUIPMENT
2

CHAPTER 2:
DEEP DIVING
EQUIPMENT

When you get involved in deep diving, you should be more selective in the equipment that you and your dive buddy use. Proper selection, adjustment, use and care of equipment is extremely important for this advanced type of diving. In this chapter we will look at how to prepare your scuba equipment for deep diving, any special equipment that is needed, and the surface support equipment that should be accessible on every deep dive.

SCUBA EQUIPMENT

Scuba diving is an equipment intensive sport. In fact, without scuba equipment, humans could not stay for prolonged periods under water. It allows us to see, breathe, and float, as well as protect us from the environment. As divers venture deeper, their scuba equipment becomes even more valuable to their comfort and safety (Figure 2-1). The greater distance between the diver and the surface increases the need for the diver to be highly skilled and able to rely on his or her own equipment, in case of an emergency.

Using a complete set of quality equipment decreases the chance of a problem occurring. In fact, today's high-quality equipment rarely malfunctions as long as it is maintained and used properly. If you are interested in learning more about equipment and how to maintain it, your local SSI Authorized Dealer offers a specialty course on Equipment Techniques. Also, your Instructor can offer an equipment consultation for you.

Figure 2-1 *As divers venture deeper, their scuba equipment becomes more valuable to their comfort and safety.*

Let us take a look at the basic pieces of equipment used on every dive, and how the demands on the equipment differ for deep diving.

Regulator

The first piece of equipment we will look at is the regulator, because it is the most sensitive and most important piece of equipment for the diver. For shallow diving, just about any regulator is adequate. However for deep diving, you should not settle for an "adequate" regulator. Deep diving requires a top-quality, high-performance regulator that will perform well at any depth (Figure 2-2). Let us quickly look at the reasons why.

Just as your air consumption increases with depth and pressure, so will breathing resistance. As the diver descends, water pressure continues to increase on the body. This pressure would make it extremely difficult, if not impossible to inhale without the aid of the much greater pressure in the intermediate stage of your regulator. When you exhale, the

Figure 2-2   *Deep diving requires a top-quality, high-performance regulator that will perform well at any depth.*

pressure in the intermediate stage of your regulator allows you to inhale against the pressure as though no external pressure existed. In fact, a high-quality balanced regulator breathes almost easier at depth than it does at the surface. There are other factors that can contribute to breathing resistance such as low tank pressure (below 500 PSI or 35 bars), rapid breathing and poor regulator maintenance. Since your tank pressure and breathing rate can be easily monitored, let us take a look at regulators—and how they perform.

Today's regulators can be purchased in one of two designs: balanced or unbalanced. For deep diving, it is recommended that your first-stage be "balanced." Balanced first-stages are slightly more expensive and are usually higher quality. A balanced first-stage is designed to maintain excellent breathing performance all the way down to very low tank pressure, while unbalanced units will become harder breathing at greater depths and at tank pressures below 600 or 700 psi (41 or 48 bars).

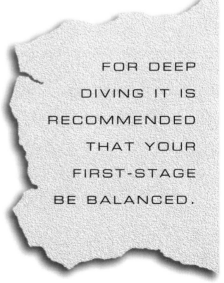

FOR DEEP DIVING IT IS RECOMMENDED THAT YOUR FIRST-STAGE BE BALANCED.

So, in summary, deep diving requires a regulator that is balanced, will give you plenty of volume at increased depth, and is easy to exhale through. The physical demands on the diver and the equipment increases with depth. An inexpensive regulator may not deliver an adequate amount of air at depth, especially when a diver becomes stressed and begins to breathe more rapidly. Your regulator should deliver all the air that two divers may need in an air-sharing situation, so both divers can breathe at the same time with separate mouthpieces (Figure 2-3).

Figure 2-3   *Your regulator should deliver all the air that two divers may need in an air-sharing situation.*

Alternate Air Source

It is tempting for many divers to buy an alternate air source of less quality since it is only a "back up" regulator. However, should you experience problems with your primary regulator, or should you need to share air at a great depth, the last thing you will want is a poor quality alternate air source. Most manufacturers offer a high quality alternate air source that will compliment your primary second-stage nicely. The most common configuration of a primary and secondary regulator is called an *octopus* (Figure 2-4).

Several manufacturers now have a unit that combines the alternate air source into the power infla-

Figure 2-4   *The most common configuration of a primary and secondary regulator is called an octopus.*

tor to create an *inflator-integrated air source* (Figure 2-5). This system eliminates one hose and makes it easy to find the extra mouthpiece in a stressful situation. No matter which system you choose, the most important aspect is that your first-stage must be of high enough quality and performance to allow two divers to share air from the same system at depth.

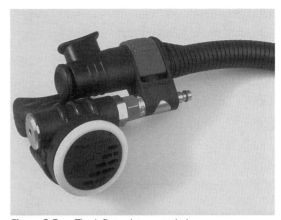

Figure 2-5 *The inflator-integrated air source combines the alternate air source into the power inflator.*

Some divers choose an *independent air source,* either in addition to one of the above systems or to stand alone as an alternate air source. The difference with this system is that it contains its own air bottle and regulator system that operate independently (Figure 2-6). Again, this system should be of high enough quality to breathe easily at depth and hold enough air to make a normal ascent to the surface from a depth of 100-130 feet (30-39 metres). It is recommended that any such system has a tank with at least 12 cubic feet of air.

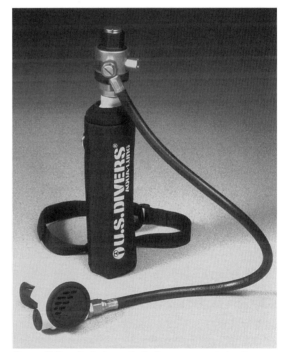

Figure 2-6 *An independant air source contains its own air bottle and regulator system that operate independently.*

Buoyancy Control Device

The next piece of equipment that is important for deep diving is the buoyancy control device or BC. Be sure that the one you select provides enough lift to bring another diver to the surface from depth. Remember, diving is equipment-intensive and a buddy sport. Each diver should wear equipment that will help a buddy in an emergency. The deeper you dive, the more critical your equipment is. It is recommended that a BC should have at least 45 pounds (20 kgs) of flotation at sea level and be equipped with a working power inflator. (Figure 2-7).

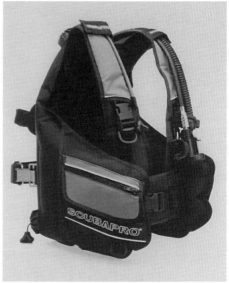

Figure 2-7 *It is recommended that a BC should have at least 45 pounds (20 kgs) of flotation at sea level and be equipped with a working power inflator.*

Tank

When selecting a tank for deep diving, you must seek a balance between a tank that supplies enough air to complete the dive safely, and a tank (usually double tanks) that has so much air that it tempts you to stay down longer than your no-decompression time limits.

As you become more comfortable with deep diving, your air consumption rate should drop and allow you to complete your dive with a 71.2 or 80 cubic foot tank (1981-2264 litres). However, if your air consumption rate is high, it may be acceptable to use double tanks or a single 95 cubic foot (2688 litres), or larger, tank for safety reasons.

Diving Instruments

Your diving instruments become much more critical to your safety when deep diving because depth, time, direction and air must be constantly monitored. The best dive plan is only as good as the follow-through. The follow-through includes making sure you do not descend deeper than your planned depth, stay down longer than your planned time, or not save enough air for your descent and safety stop and still have a 500 PSI (35 bar) safety margin.

■ Depth Gauges:

Your instruments should be of high quality and properly maintained. The most accurate analog gauges at depth are the oil-filled, the gas-filled and the bourdon tube. However, no analog gauge will be completely accurate at depth, and it should be recalibrated annually to ensure its accuracy. It is recommended that deep divers carry more than one style. This allows you to compare your gauges at shallow depths, such as when you are making your 15 foot (5 metre) safety stop.

Figure 2-8 *Electronic gauges are more accurate than analog gauges, and the only maintenance they require is new batteries.*

Electronic gauges are also available that display your depth, pressure and other information digitally. These consoles may, or may not, include a dive computer. Equipment manufacturers claim that electronic gauges are more accurate than analog gauges and the only maintenance they require is new batteries (Figure 2-8).

No matter which style you chose, make sure the gauge has a maximum depth indicator so you have a record of the deepest point you reached during your dive. This number must be used when figuring any repetitive dive plans.

■ Submersible Pressure Gauges:

Your SPG is also an important part of the instrument console. As with depth gauges, the SPG can be either analog or digital. Your pressure gauge needs to be as accurate as possible, so you should check it periodically by comparing it to another gauge. You can do this by hooking up one gauge after the other to the same tank of air.

■ Compass:

A compass is valuable in deep diving because you must be able to navigate accurately back to the point where you will begin your ascent to the 15 foot (5 metre) safety stop. This is particularly important when boat diving, or when diving at night or in limited visibility. As with all your other instruments, your compass should be of high quality. To learn more about compasses, ask your local SSI Authorized Dealer about a specialty course on Navigation.

■ **Timing Device:** Because bottom time is not flexible when deep diving, an accurate timing device must be used. One type of timing device is the wrist watch. It should have a uni-directional bezel that can be set to indicate the start of the dive. Digital watches are also popular, as well as digital bottom timers. These dive timers can be attached to your console, or may be part of your digital instruments or computer. The advantage of a digital bottom timer when deep diving is that you do not have to remember to set it or turn it on, it does so automatically by reacting to water and pressure.

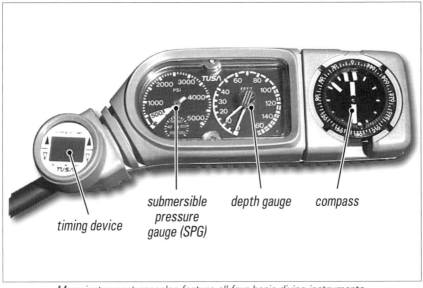

timing device   submersible   depth gauge   compass
                 pressure
                 gauge (SPG)

Many instrument consoles feature all four basic diving instruments.

Exposure Suit

Cold water hastens the onset of nitrogen narcosis and decompression sickness, two potential hazards when deep diving. You may need a thicker wet suit, or even a dry suit, due to the drop in water temperature at increased depth at some dive sites. You may also need to add a hood, gloves, or a vest (Figure 2-9). Keeping warm is essential when deep diving, because a loss of body heat uses energy and impairs your ability to think clearly. Also, as water pressure increases, your wet suit compresses, thereby causing it to lose some insulation at depth. A wet suit you can wear comfortably at 60 feet (18 metres) may not be warm enough at 120 feet (36 metres). Remember, as your wet suit compresses you will also lose buoyancy.

When using a dry suit, it is the undergarment that actually provides warmth in cold water. The dry suit itself may keep you dry, but it provides no insulation from the cold. Before using a dry suit you should read the owner's manual and follow the manufacturer's guidelines. It is recommended that you take an orientation to dry suit diving or a specialty course in *Dry Suit Diving.*

Figure 2-9   *Due to the drop in water temperature at increased depth, you may need to add a hood, gloves, or a vest.*

SPECIAL EQUIPMENT

Now that we have discussed all the basic pieces of scuba equipment that are required on *every* dive (not just every *deep* dive), let us go on and analyze the equipment that has special applications to deep diving.

Diving Computer

Although the diving computer is an option for deep divers, it is highly recommended; those who use them on a regular basis consider them mandatory. These units are used to monitor your no-decompression limits, or to advise you what depth to stop at if you inadvertently get into a decompression situation. Most computers give you depth, bottom time, an ascent alarm if you are exceeding the proper ascent rate, remaining no-decompression time, a memory for divelog information, your surface interval between dives, scrolling for no-decompression limits for the next dive and, in some models, the water temperature and tank pressure.

Some computer manufacturers have recommendations for computer failure, as does the AAUS, American Academy of Underwater Sciences (see Appendix). In the event of computer failure, most recommend that divers surface using normal ascent procedures. It is not safe to switch to the dive tables without backup instruments and an up-to-date DiveLog. See Chapter 5 for more information on computer failure.

The benefit of a diving computer is that it increases your bottom time by giving you credit for all the time that you spend at shallower depths (Figure 2-10). This is handy when multi-level diving. If you are doing a "bounce dive," or simply dropping to your deepest depth and then ascending, a computer will not be any more helpful. As with all specialized pieces of equipment, you should receive additional training in how to use a computer before diving with one. You will also need to learn about how your particular model of computer operates because they all offer different features. If you are interested in learning more about computers, ask your local SSI store about a Computer Diving Specialty course. ***Note: Each diver must be equipped with his or her own computer. Computers should not be shared while diving.***

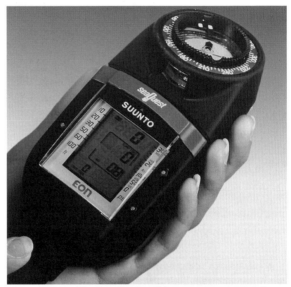

Figure 2-10 *The benefit of a diving computer is that it increases your bottom time by giving you credit for all the time that you spent at shallower depths.*

Lights

Because water gets darker at depth, a dive light may help to read gauges, to signal your buddy, or simply to restore color to the marine life (Figure 2-11). You

COMPUTERS SHOULD NOT BE SHARED WHILE DIVING.

should carry a large primary light as well as a smaller backup light that can be stored in a BC pocket or attached to a BC strap. Be sure both lights are fully charged or have fresh batteries before each dive. The light should also be equipped with a lanyard that

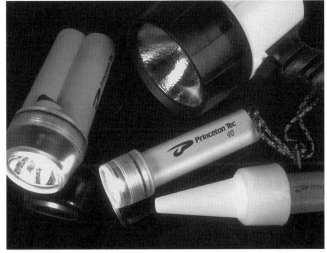

Figure 2-11   *Because water gets darker at depth, a dive light may be helpful to read gauges, signal your buddy, or simply to restore color to the marine life.*

can be secured to your wrist.

You and your buddy may also want to attach a chemical glow stick to your tank for emergency purposes, in case you should happen to get separated under water or on the surface. Another good habit is to mark the ascent/descent line with a strobe light so it can be easily seen from some distance away, even in poor visibility.

Dive Tables and Slate

You may want to carry your submersible, plastic dive tables on every dive. This allows you to do contingency planning under water should your dive plan change. You should also write your dive plan on a slate that is carried with you. The slate can also be used to refigure your dive plan, record your compass setting, and for communication with your buddy. Securely attach the slate to your BC so it is easily accessible and cannot be lost, yet stays out of your way.

Knife

A knife can be a valuable tool on your dive should you become entangled in a net, rope, fishing line, kelp, or any other material. Your buddy can easily assist in freeing you if he or she has a knife. If not, valuable bottom time can be wasted in attempting to become untangled, not to mention the obvious safety concerns.

Spare Parts and Repair Kit

Because properly maintained equipment is so important to deep diving, last minute adjustments or field repairs may be necessary to prevent having to cancel a dive due to equipment problems. A complete spare parts and repair kit can come in handy for both your and your buddy's equipment, or any fellow divers in need.

SURFACE SUPPORT

> **NOTE:** THE FOLLOWING SUPPORT EQUIPMENT AND PERSONNEL ARE RECOMMENDED FOR DEEP DIVING. THE FINAL DECISION ON THE USE OF SURFACE SUPPORT SHOULD BE MADE BY THE BUDDY TEAM AND THE DIVING INSTRUCTOR, IF APPROPRIATE.

In addition to the equipment you need for your dive, you must also consider what surface support equipment to use. This additional equipment should be available if, by chance, some sort of accident should occur. Due to the nature of deep diving, accidents are, unfortunately, a concern, so it is prudent to be prepared.

Surface support includes not only equipment, but also personnel and an accident management plan. Let us take a look at some of the recommended surface support you should prepare for each deep dive. Remember, the deeper you are diving, and the more hazardous the conditions, the more important surface support will be to your safety.

Support Personnel

When deep diving, one member of the dive group should always be left on the

Figure 2-12 *When deep diving, one member of the group should always be on the surface.*

surface. This person can assist in entries and exits, radio for help, or offer aid to divers who need help on the surface (Fig-ure 2-12). If you are diving on a charter boat or with a group, the boat captain or group leader may stay on the boat. If you are diving with your friends, one of the group should take turns as the support person. Either way, this person should be a competent individual who knows how to use the emergency equipment and communications system, and if boat diving, how to operate the boat and anchor.

Descent/Ascent Line

A stable ascent/descent line is a valuable diving tool, especially when diving off a boat or in limited visibility. When diving, a line helps you make a more controlled ascent and descent. This line can either be the anchor line of the boat, or a weighted drop line that is either attached to the boat, or a float on the surface that is weighted or attached to the bottom.

Safety Stop Tank and Line

When deep diving, it is a good idea to have an extra tank with two second stages tied off at 15 feet (5 metres) to a separate safety line, or to the ascent line (Figure 2-13). Before the dive, be sure to check the pressure in the tank, and then turn the air off before tying it off under water. Do not count on using this air as part of your dive plan, it is there for emergency use should you run low on air during your safety stop. Proper planning and execution should prevent this situation.

When boat diving, tie the ascent/descent line off mid-ship and tie the extra tank to it. The line should be weighted so it hangs straight down. You may want to put some extra weights on the line in case you or your buddy are too positively buoyant at the end of the dive. Do not use an anchor line or a line tied off the back of the boat,

Figure 2-13   *When deep diving, it is a good idea to have an extra tank with two second stages tied off at 15 feet (5 metres).*

because the wave action will not allow you to hang at a constant depth of 15 feet (5 metres). If deep diving from a boat, be sure to have rapid transportation to shore in case of an emergency, and the ability to radio for help.

When diving from shore, you can use some type of surface flotation that the descent line can be tied to. The descent line float should be able to support the weight of all the divers while they are making the 15 foot (5 metre) safety stop.

Surface Marker

A surface marker that the underwater team can use to signal the support personnel on the surface, if assistance is needed under water, should also be set. A surface marker can simply be a float with a line and weight attached to it (Figure 2-14). Attached to this line should be a slate and pencil that the divers can use to write a message on. By tugging on the line, the support people can see the float on the surface move and know to pull up the line and get the message off the slate. This can come in handy if extra tanks or weights are needed for the safety stop, or if some other sort of emer-gency has taken place.

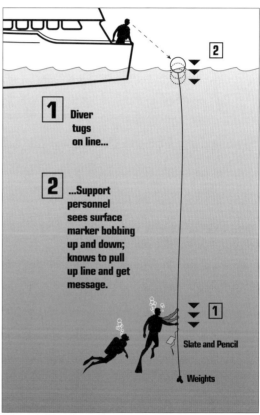

1 Diver tugs on line...

2 ...Support personnel sees surface marker bobbing up and down; knows to pull up line and get message.

Slate and Pencil

Weights

Figure 2-14 *Deep divers can utilize the surface marker to signal the support personnel when they need help.*

Oxygen

Regardless of where you deep dive, be sure to have an adequate supply of 100% oxygen easily accessible in case of a diving emergency. It has been proven that 100% oxygen is effective first aid for diving accidents. More information on the use of oxygen is available from the

SSI Stress and Rescue program. The Divers Alert Network offers a course, *Oxygen First Aid in Diving Accidents*, in the United States if you are interested in becoming trained in oxygen management.

First Aid Kit

A professional-grade First Aid kit with all the required contents should also be available at the dive site, or on the boat. A good First Aid manual is also a necessity. It is recommended that all divers receive first aid and CPR training. Your local SSI Dealer may offer SSI/NSC training in first aid and CPR.

Radio/Communications

If you are boat diving, a radio should be available to call for transport or assistance in case of an emergency (Figure 2-15). If you are shore diving, a telephone should be nearby, or a portable telephone or radio should be taken with you to the site.

Figure 2-15   *If you are boat diving, a radio should be available to call for transport or help in case of an emergency.*

Accident Management Plan

An accident management plan not only includes having the necessary equipment available, but it also includes having the proper training and access to emergency medical personnel. Your plan should include the phone/radio numbers of the nearest emergency medical service (EMS). It is also a good idea to let your buddy know about your past medical history which may be of interest to medical personnel, such as previous decompression sickness, blood sugar disorders, recent surgery and drug allergies. All this information should be kept accessible. You might want to affix it to the inside of your log book and let your buddy know about it.

Deep diving requires proper training, proper equipment, and proper dive execution. Using the best equipment in the world will not make deep diving safer unless you know how to use it properly. The best training in the world will not suffice unless you use proper equipment and execute the dive plan properly.

When you participate in advanced diving activities, the equipment you use should be of the highest quality available and exceed all performance requirements of the dive objective. Remember, good surface support equipment is essential for deep diving activities.

Now that we have looked at dive planning and the equipment needed for deep diving, let us go on to Chapter 3 and look at how to execute the dive.

CHAPTER 2
REVIEW

1. Deep diving requires a top-quality, high-performance _____ that will perform well at any depth.

2. A _____ first-stage is designed to maintain excellent breathing performance all the way down to very low tank pressure.

3. The most accurate analog gauges at depth are the oil-filled, the gas-filled, and the _____ _____.

4. Equipment manufacturers claim that _____ gauges are more accurate than analog gauges and the only maintenance they require is new batteries.

5. The benefit of a diving computer is that it increases your _____ _____ by giving you _____ for all the time you spend at shallower depths.

6. When deep diving, one member of the dive group should always be left on the _____. This person can assist in entries and exits, radio for help, or offer aid to divers who need help on the surface.

7. When deep diving, it is a good idea to have an extra tank with two second-stages tied off at _____ _____ to a separate _____ _____ , or to the ascent line.

8. An accident management plan includes having the necessary equipment available, but it also includes having the proper _____, and access to emergency _____ _____.

THE DIVE

3

CHAPTER 3:
THE DIVE

Now we have had a chance to look at pre-dive planning and the equipment you will need for deep diving, let us look at actually planning and executing a deep dive. The skills for deep diving vary little from your Open Water Diver course, however, they need to be executed more precisely. Buoyancy control, ascents, and descents should be executed with the utmost control and precision. Plus, you need to be studiously observant of your time, depth, direction and air consumption, as well as your own physical state and that of all team members.

PRE-ENTRY PROCEDURES

The deep diving process begins before the diver ever enters the water. Deep diving is all about planning, and then rechecking everything to minimize the chance of something going wrong (Figure 3-1). As we mentioned in the first two chapters, making a dive plan and preparing your equipment are critical to the deep diving process. *Plan your dive; dive your plan!*

The preparation does not end here, however. In fact, it does not stop until the diver is safely under the water, and the dive is under way. Let us quickly look at the pre-entry procedures for deep diving.

Figure 3-1 *Deep diving is all about planning, and then rechecking everything to minimize the chance of something going wrong.*

PLAN
YOUR
DIVE;
DIVE
YOUR
PLAN!

Planning No-Decompression Dives

The first step in the diving process is always to make a dive plan. All deep dives should be planned within the Doppler no-decompression limits.

Let us review a few basic points about dive planning. When planning your maximum depth, remember to use the exact depth listed on the dive tables or, if it is between, round it up to the next greatest number. For example, if you are planning a dive to 85 feet (25.5 metres) which is the bottom, then you would round your depth up to 90 feet (27 metres).

If you are planning on making a repetitive dive, there are a few basic rules you will need to follow; always make the deepest dive first, and pre-plan both dives to ensure you will have enough bottom time left to complete your second dive (Figure 3-2). For example, if you do not take the time to plan through your second dive, you may find that you will need a surface interval of almost 6 hours in order to make two 100 foot (30 metre) dives in one day. If you do not plan ahead, you may end up making your second dive to only 40 feet (12 metres).

The planning stage is more than a time to make a dive profile, however, it is a time for buddies to talk about hand signals, to learn about each others equipment and how it functions, and to discuss important topics such as a lost buddy procedure. For example, you should know how your buddy's power inflator operates and what kind of alternate air source

Figure 3-2 *If you are planning on making a repetitive dive, always make the deepest dive first, and pre-plan both dives to ensure you will have enough bottom time.*

he has in case of an emergency. The more thorough the plan, the higher the comfort level on the dive. Remember, do not plan a dive deeper than a buddy team member has been certified to, or feels comfortable doing.

Getting Ready

The dressing stage is important because it allows the diver to re-analyze his or her equipment and make sure it is functioning properly. It also allows you to make any last minute adjustments to equipment to make sure it fits more comfortably. This stage is also an indicator of the diver's stress level. Any discomfort will probably surface in the form of stalling, preoccupation, irritability, frustration and difficulty with equipment. Any abnormal behavior should be addressed, and the diver should be allowed to cancel the dive if necessary. More information on stress can be learned in a *Diver Stress and Rescue* course, available at your local SSI Authorized Dealer.

Proper Weighting

Proper weighting and buoyancy control are two important skills for diving comfort—especially at depth. For when you dive deep, the water pressure will greatly reduce the buoyancy in your wet suit and BC as the air inside them compresses. This will make you negatively buoyant at depth. So why not just take some weight off your weight belt? The problem is, although you may be negative at depth, as you surface with lower tank pressure you become positively buoyant, some-times too buoyant to make a normal ascent or to stop at 15 feet (5 metres) for a safety stop. This is very dangerous when deep diving. The key is proper weighting at the surface, before you make your dive, and proper buoyancy adjustment during the dive.

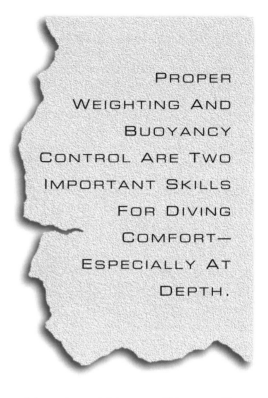

PROPER WEIGHTING AND BUOYANCY CONTROL ARE TWO IMPORTANT SKILLS FOR DIVING COMFORT— ESPECIALLY AT DEPTH.

You may have already learned how to weight yourself in your Open Water Diver course, however, when you were only diving in shallow water for training, it was acceptable to weight yourself neutral on the surface. For deep diving, you will need to start slightly negative and take other factors into consideration such as tank buoyancy, because the buoyancy of a tank can vary drastically from when it is full to when it is low. For example, an aluminum 80 (2264 litres) may be 2 pounds (.9 kgs) negative when it is full at the surface, but be 4 pounds (1.8 kgs) positive at the end of the dive when it is almost empty. In contrast, a 71.2 cubic foot (2015 litres) steel tank is approximately 11 pounds (5 kgs) negative when it is full, and remains 5-6 pounds (2.2-2.7 kgs) negative when it is empty. You can see how tank buoyancy can dramatically affect your weighting at the beginning and end of a dive. In both examples, there is a 6 pound (2.7 kg) difference from the beginning to the end. You will need to adjust for this increased buoyancy by adding enough weight at the beginning of the dive, so you are still neutral at the end for the 15 foot (5 metre) stop.

Another way to perfect your weighting is to keep a precise record in the SSI DiveLog for each dive, whether it was in fresh or salt water, what type of exposure suit was worn, what type of tank was used, and how much weight you used. At the end of the dive, record whether you were neutral, negative or positive during your 15 foot safety stop. After experimenting on numerous dives, you will have a good record to begin referring to for future dives. You can record this information on the Proper Weighting Tables in your SSI DiveLog. Because a diver's body composition and comfort level affect weighting, there is no exact formula for how much weight to add for each type of tank. Use the buoyancy chart in the appendix as a guideline, or ask your SSI Authorized Dealer about the buoyancy information for your tank.

Pre-Entry Buddy Check

Once you and your buddy are dressed, properly weighted and ready, perform a pre-entry buddy check. This check may detect potential problems such as tangled hoses, loose weight belts, or low tank pressure. Quickly recheck each others equipment and reconfirm important parts of the dive plan. Once again, either diver should feel comfortable canceling the dive at this point if they are uncomfortable.

Surface Procedures

After you and your buddy enter the water, take a moment to become acclimated to the water and to orient yourself. Swim to the descent line if one is available, and reconfirm your compass heading if necessary. Once you are both comfortable, record the time on your slate, set your bottom timer or watch, and descend.

DESCENT PROCEDURES

Descent procedures should be discussed during the pre-dive process if they will vary from a standard descent. For example, this may include when more than two divers are diving together, or when a line is not going to be used.

Proper descent procedures include going down feet first, with the power inflator in your left hand while facing your buddy (Figure 3-3— see page 44). You must remain aware of your buddy's needs at all times, and be on the lookout for general problems Your descent rate should not exceed your comfort level, or a maximum rate of 75 feet (22.5 metres) per minute. Experts agree that this is as fast as the average diver can descend without experiencing potential problems. Faster descents may cause squeezes, disorientation or an out-of-control situation. The diver should be able to stop at any time, and must avoid a "crash landing" on the bottom that can damage the reef or your equipment, or ruin the visibility.

Again, proper weighting is another important part of the descent procedures. You must be heavy enough to make a controlled descent, without being so heavy that you cannot compensate with your BC to slow your descent if needed. This is why a line is helpful when descending. The diver can slow down if necessary, stop to equalize ears, readjust a piece of equipment, or check on his or her buddy. You can also make a descent using a wall, kelp or the slope of the beach.

Figure 3-3 *Proper descent procedures include going down feet first, with the power inflator in your left hand, while facing your buddy.*

DEEP DIVING PROCEDURES

Deep diving procedures do not vary dramatically from normal diving procedures, except that divers must be more aware of their own comfort level as well as their buddy's, and they must monitor their equipment more closely.

Once you and your buddy reach your planned depth, take a moment to orient yourselves and to make sure you are both "ok" before swimming off. Because of the increased pressure at depth, your sensations may change, so take time to let them adjust. For example, the air in your tank may taste different and your exhaust bubbles may sound different. You may also feel different due to the effects of nitrogen narcosis. These and other deep diving hazards will be discussed in the next chapter. The last thing you should do is to check your air pressure and your weight belt. Because of the increased pressure, your suit will compress and your weight belt may loosen up.

Controlling Your Buoyancy

As we discussed earlier in Proper Weighting, one of the major differences of diving at depth will be your ability to control your buoyancy (Figure 3-4). Your wet suit will compress at depth and lose some of its buoyancy, and the volume of air in your BC will continue to decrease as pressure increases. Both factors will influence the need to inflate the BC slightly more at depth in order to remain neutrally buoyant. Inflate the BC in small increments, letting the increased air take effect before you continue to inflate. If you over inflate, you will find yourself beginning to rise and then having to immediately deflate your BC again. Continuous adjustments to your BC at depth may

Figure 3-4 *One of the major differences of diving at depth will be your ability to control your buoyancy.*

lead to unstable buoyancy control. A small adjustment is all that is needed. Keep in mind that there is a delay in the time it takes for the BC to change your buoyancy at increased depth.

Monitoring Your Gauges

Because depth, bottom time and air supply are so important to deep diving, you should continually monitor your gauges. You should make sure that you do not stay down longer or dive any deeper than you had planned, and that you begin your ascent before you reach your minimum air pressure.

Failure to monitor your gauges could lead to an inadvertent decompression or a low air situation. When you dive deep, dive smart and stick to your plan.

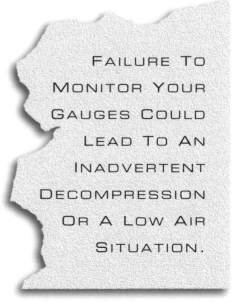

FAILURE TO MONITOR YOUR GAUGES COULD LEAD TO AN INADVERTENT DECOMPRESSION OR A LOW AIR SITUATION.

Orientation and Navigation

It is extremely important to know where your exit point is at all times during the dive. In tropical water with near-infinite visibility, this is usually not difficult. However, current, kelp, and similar-looking reef formations can disorient you. In turbid water and on night dives, you often cannot see more than a few feet, and on deep dives, surfacing to determine your location is impractical. You must be able to find your way to the ascent line so you can make your safety stop. If your air should begin to run low, it is important that you can find the ascent line.

If you are comfortable using natural navigation, be sure and note any landmarks or reference points that will lead you back to the ascent line. If the visibility does not lend itself to natural navigation, or if you feel more comfortable using a compass, be sure to take a heading before you enter the water, and constantly monitor the compass to make sure you stay on course (Figure 3-5). If you are boat diving where there is a current, you may want to take your compass heading in the direction of the anchor line. This way, if you cannot find the anchor line when it is time to ascend you can swim into your compass heading (into the current), do your 15 foot (5 metre) safety stop in mid-water, and still surface in front of the boat. This can help prevent drifting down current from the boat.

Navigation skills are important to all divers; if you are not familiar or not comfortable with navigation techniques, you should take a Navigation Specialty course from your SSI Dealer.

Figure 3-5   *You may want to take a compass heading for your destination before entering the water, just as a back up.*

Communicating With Your Buddy

You and your buddy should stay in constant communication when deep diving. Communication increases your comfort level, and allows you to spot any problems in your buddy or relay any problems you may be having. Monitor yourself and your buddy for the effects of nitrogen narcosis which will be discussed in the next chapter.

Lost Buddy Procedure

Buddies should always stay within an arms reach of each other; but, due to unforeseen circumstances you and your buddy may get separated under water. A lost buddy procedure should be discussed in the planning phase so each dive buddy will know what actions to take. A recommended procedure is to return to the ascent line immediately upon separation, and then wait for a reasonable amount of time before ascending for help. How long you wait will depend on your depth, your air supply, your

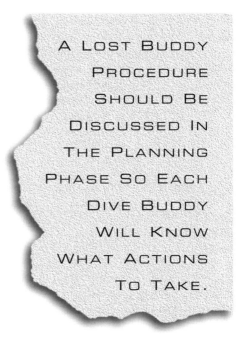

A LOST BUDDY PROCEDURE SHOULD BE DISCUSSED IN THE PLANNING PHASE SO EACH DIVE BUDDY WILL KNOW WHAT ACTIONS TO TAKE.

available bottom time, and the urgency of the situation. If your buddy is in danger, you will want to get help as quickly as possible.

If your buddy is not waiting for you on the surface, you should instigate search procedures. It is not advisable for you to aid in the search if it could put you in danger of decompression sickness. You must weigh the risk/benefit of the situation before getting back into the water. The safety support personnel on the boat should make the search, or you should radio for help. These emergencies are why you arrange for support people and equipment. It is not worth risking one life for another, especially if it is possible to get outside help.

ASCENT PROCEDURES

Before it is time to ascend, return to the ascent line and your exit point. If you are diving in limited visibility or an unfamiliar area, a compass is handy to help find the ascent line. You do not want to get lost at 100 feet or 30 metres when your air is running low.

The first step to a proper ascent is knowing when to ascend. When deep diving, your air supply must be constantly monitored so you have adequate air for a slow ascent and a long safety stop, while still reaching the surface with a 500 psi/35 bar reserve. There is a formula you can use to help ensure that you will have an adequate air supply for your ascent:

for every 10 feet (3 metres) you must ascend, reserve 100 pounds of air (7 bars). For example, this means that if you are diving at 100 feet (30 metres), you will need to allow 1000 psi (68 bars) of air for the ascent and safety stop. When you add your 500 psi reserve to the 1000 psi, this means you must begin your ascent when you are down to 1500 psi. Because this formula is conservative, it should work for even the fastest breathers. However, it is only a guideline; you may need to adjust the formula to fit your breathing pattern.

When it is time for you and your buddy to ascend, start by quickly checking each other and your equipment to make sure all is "ok." When the team is ready to ascend, you and your buddy should face each other and start a controlled ascent at a rate of 30 feet or 9 metres per minute (Figure 3-6). If a line is used, hold it in one hand and your gauges in the other, you can monitor your rate of ascent and slow it down if necessary. A 30 foot (9 metre) per minute ascent rate means that you will ascend 10 feet (3 metres) every 20 seconds. Use caution when you get about 40 feet or 12 metres from the surface, because the air in your BC will be expanding to a volume that can make you become out-of-control and be at the surface before you know it.

Figure 3-6   *When the team is ready to ascend, you and your buddy should face each other and start a controlled ascent at a rate of 30 feet (9 metres) per minute.*

Most divers, even those with a lot of experience, have very poor buoyancy control during descent, during the dive, and during the ascent. Buoyancy control is the single most important skill for divers to master.

You and your buddy should be within an arms length of each other during the ascent in case you need to help each other, and whenever possible, use an ascent line. You can also make an ascent using a wall, kelp, or the slope of a beach so you have both a visual reference point, and something to grab onto if you begin ascending out of control.

It will be easier to control your ascent if you gently kick to the surface, rather than floating up as your BC inflates. As mentioned earlier, the air in your BC will expand upon ascent, causing you to vent air from it rather than inflate it (Figure 3-7).

If you are diving from a boat, it may have a safety stop bar that hangs at 15 feet (5 metres) below the boat. A bar is nice because it allows a group of divers to make a safety stop all at once. It can be difficult to hover at 15 feet (5 metres) without a line, even if you have excellent buoyancy control.

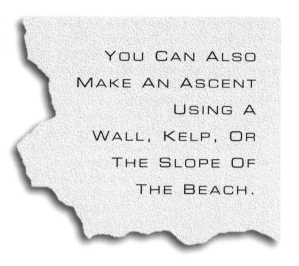

YOU CAN ALSO MAKE AN ASCENT USING A WALL, KELP, OR THE SLOPE OF THE BEACH.

Figure 3-7 *The air in your BC will expand upon ascent, causing you to vent air from it, rather than inflate it.*

The current or surge can cause you to drift away from your exit point, and make you tread water to stay in place. An ascent line provides stability and control for deep divers. If you are diving in an area with a shallow coral reef or kelp bed, you can also end your dive by exploring this shallow area instead of making a safety stop. This can be a lot more interesting than hanging on a line, as long as you maintain a depth of approximately 15 feet. No matter what method you choose, you should make a safety stop at 15 feet (5 metres) for 3 to 5 minutes after diving deep (Figure 3-8). The value of the 3-5 minute safety stop came out of the workshop held by the American Academy of Underwater Sciences in 1989, and at that time was shown to help lower the chances of decompression sickness.

Figure 3-8 *You should make a safety stop at 15 feet (5 meters) for 3 to 5 minutes after diving deep.*

Some deep, wreck divers carry an emergency line with them which is called an "up-line." Should a diver not be able to find or return to the anchor line for the ascent, the diver can hook the up-line to the wreck and ascend from this point. When the diver reaches 15 feet (5 metres) for the safety stop, the up-line will allow them to maintain this exact depth because of the tension created between the wreck and the positively buoyant diver (Figure 3-9). SSI Dealers that specialize in wreck diving can assist you in how to use an up-line.

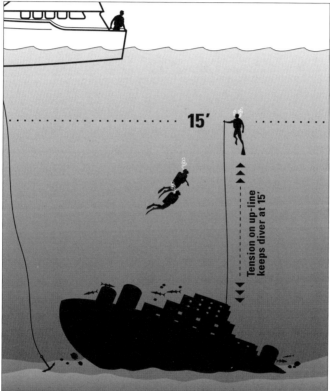

Figure 3-9 *When the diver reaches 15 feet (5 metres) for the safety stop, the up-line will allow them to maintain this exact depth because of the tension created between the wreck and the positively buoyant diver.*

Deep diving can be a safe and exciting activity through proper planning, preparation and execution. Deep diving requires constant monitoring of your buoyancy, gauges, and your own and your buddy's physical state. As we have mentioned many times, there is less room for error when diving at depth. Deep diving also introduces certain hazards due to the increased pressure at depth. Let us move on to Chapter 4 and look at these Increased Hazards of Deep Diving.

CHAPTER 3
REVIEW

1. All deep dives should be planned within the

_____ _____ – _____

limits.

2. For deep diving, you will need to start slightly
_____ and take other factors into
consideration such as _____ buoyancy,
because the buoyancy of a tank can vary drastically from when it is full, to when it is low.

3. Your descent rate should not exceed your comfort level, or a maximum rate of ____ _____
per minute.

4. Continuous adjustments to your BC at depth
may lead to _____ buoyancy control.

5. If you are diving in limited visibility or in an
unfamiliar area, a _____ is handy to
help find the ascent line.

6. There is a formula you can use to help ensure that you will have an adequate air supply for your ascent: for every 10 feet (3 metres) you must ascend, reserve _____ _____ of air.

7. A 30 foot-per-minute (9 metres) ascent rate means that you will ascend 10 feet (3 metres) every _____ seconds.

8. You can also make an ascent using a wall, kelp, or the slope of a beach so you have both a _____ _____ _____ , and something to grab onto if you begin ascending out of control.

Increased
Hazards
Of Deep Diving

4

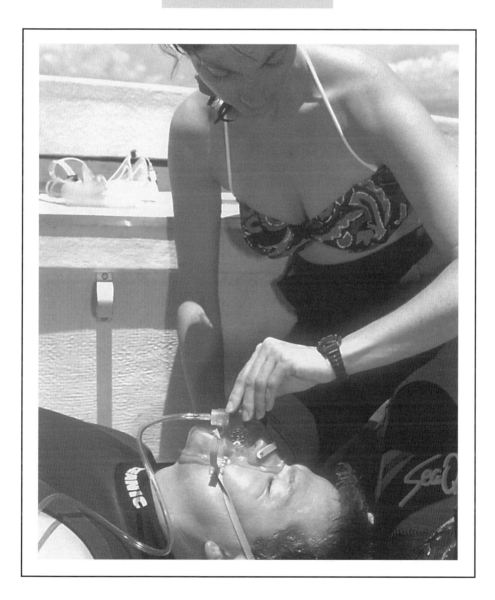

CHAPTER 4:
INCREASED HAZARDS OF DEEP DIVING

Because of the nature of deep diving, and the effects of pressure, deep divers will always be at an increased risk for problems and accidents. This risk will be lessened through education, and by understanding the potential hazards a deep diver may encounter. This increased knowledge allows a diver to plan ahead, and to know what signs and symptoms to look for to avoid an accident.

In this chapter we will look at the increased hazards of deep diving and how to minimize them. We will also look at accident management, and what steps a diver should take should an accident occur.

POTENTIAL HAZARDS

Not all potential hazards are life threatening or dangerous, however, they can be serious enough to require cancellation of the dive. If not dealt with immediately, they may escalate into a serious problem.

Nitrogen Narcosis

High concentrations of nitrogen under pressure have a narcotic effect on humans. It can create an abnormal sense of euphoria and well-being, nervous symptoms, and a slowing down or dulling of the normal functions of the brain. It is not known exactly why nitrogen has this effect. A diver who is "narced" may have difficulty doing things that would normally be easy, such as reading instruments, making decisions, operating a BC, or communicating with a buddy. Nitrogen narcosis can cause dizziness or disorientation, and if the diver continues to descend, eventual unconsciousness.

> NITROGEN NARCOSIS CAN CAUSE DIZZINESS OR DISORIENTATION, AND IF THE DIVER CONTINUES TO DESCEND, EVENTUAL UNCONSCIOUSNESS.

Some divers experience mild symptoms of narcosis at depths as shallow as 60 feet (18 metres), while some divers do not seem to be seriously affected at great depths. There is no time element involved in the onset of narcosis. Symptoms can occur immediately at depth, or can wait until the dive is well under way.

Most deep diving experts agree that it is possible for humans to "adapt" to the effects of nitrogen narcosis by working up to greater depths through repeated exposures. However, a diver's susceptibility may change from day to day or from dive to dive. It is impossible to predict whether you will be affected, and if so, to what degree.

Should you experience any unusual feelings at depth, signal your buddy, and ascend until the feelings dissipate. By ascending to a lesser depth, you lower the partial pressure of the nitrogen and the symptoms go away. After the symptoms are gone, you may want to try going back down. Quite often, the diver will not experience narcosis at the same depth the second time. However, when going back down, be sure not to violate the depth or bottom time of the planned dive. Stay close to your buddy, should you need assistance, and be prepared to ascend immediately if narcosis reoccurs. *Do not attempt to descend again if your buddy is not near you, watching you, or able to assist you.*

Whenever a diver gives the "up" signal, both buddies should respond by starting up. Do not take time at the bottom to ask why; just go up. After ascending a few feet, you can stop and communicate with your buddy. Remember, any diver may abort a dive at any time. This is why it is important to dive with buddies of similar experience and ability.

The effects of narcosis may be minimized by staying in good physical condition, eating a well-balanced diet, getting plenty of rest, and maintaining a regular exercise schedule.

Generally there are no after-effects of nitrogen narcosis, however, some deep divers have reported that the symptoms of narcosis did not wear off immediately. This may be a post-traumatic experience.

Carbon Dioxide Excess

Carbon dioxide (CO_2) excess is generally caused by unintentionally hyperventilating through shallow, rapid breathing while scuba diving. It can also be a result of a hard-breathing regulator, or just diver fatigue. If CO_2 excess does occur, you should *stop, breathe, think and act* to prevent stress from occurring (Figure 4-1). Repeat this procedure over and over in your mind until it becomes a conditioned automatic response. Just relax and get control of your breathing by inhaling and exhaling deeply.

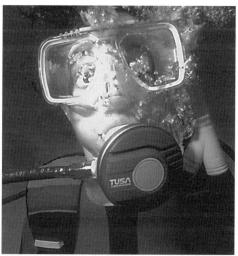

Figure 4-1 *If CO_2 excess does occur, you should* **stop, breathe, think** *and* **act** *to prevent stress from occurring.*

The symptoms of CO_2 excess are lightheadedness, an inability to think clearly, a feeling of not being able to breathe, and a dull headache. A sharp headache is most likely due to the effects of cold water. More severe symptoms include a loss of consciousness and possible convulsions. Treatment for severe CO_2 excess includes getting the victim to the surface as quickly as possible.

Fatigue

Mental and physical fatigue are two of the least talked about causes of diving accidents. In deep diving, it is very important not to allow yourself or your buddy to dive, or to continue the dive, if you do not feel well — both mentally and physically. One way to minimize fatigue is to gradually work down to the greater depths with a deep diving instructor.

Other causes of fatigue when diving include lack of sleep, illness, cold water, water movements such as currents, excessive drag from equipment, being overweighted, and overworking.

Hypothermia

Hypothermia is generally defined as the condition of having one's body temperature fall below normal. The term is also used to describe the overall effects of severe cold on a victim, whether it is under water or on the surface. Since the water temperature can dramatically drop at depth, especially in lakes or smaller bodies of water, hypothermia can pose a number of problems for deep divers. It is important to wear the proper exposure suit for the water temperature of the depth you will be diving (Figure 4-2).

Figure 4-2   *Be sure to wear the proper exposure suit for the water temperature of the depth you will be diving.*

The symptoms of hypothermia include shivering, impaired ability to perform tasks, loss of dexterity in the hands, lack of coordination, a dulling of the senses, and a lowered ability to think clearly.

If you become chilled during the dive, it is all right to do mild exercises, like swimming while under water, to warm up. However, should you continue to be chilled, you should cancel the dive and get out of the water as exercise will actually accelerate the onset of hypothermia.

Should you or your buddy become mildly hypothermic, warm yourself slowly by getting into dry clothes and into a warm environment. Do not give a hypothermia victim anything to eat or drink unless he or she is fully conscious, and then, only administer non-caffeinated or non-alcoholic fluids. If symptoms are severe or if the victim is unconscious, get the diver to an emergency medical facility immediately for rewarming.

DIVING MALADIES

In addition to the potential hazards already discussed, the more severe diving maladies that are a potential hazard on *every* dive, become a real danger on deep dives. This is not to say that there is a high frequency of accidents on deep dives. There is, however, an increased risk of accident. Let us look at the diving maladies that can affect deep divers, so we may learn to prevent them before they occur.

Decompression Sickness

Decompression sickness, commonly called "DCS" or "the bends," is also known as Cassion's Disease. When deep diving, DCS is usually caused by staying too long at depth or an improper ascent rate. A diver can also have a physiological problem that hinders the nitrogen desaturation. Keep in mind that all divers risk the bends, even when making no-decompression dives within the Doppler limits of the U.S. Navy tables, or when using decompression computers. The risk of getting the bends is also increased with deep diving.

Researchers have found in recent years that there are certain factors that make people at increased risk of the bends. Decompression sickness research is still in its infancy stage. Each year, new information is compiled through the Divers Alert Network. They collect accident statistics that are used to find correlations between accident victims. Through this research they have compiled a list of factors that increase the risk of DCS:

Decompression Sickness Risk Factors:

- Age (usually over 40)
- Poor physical condition
- Obesity
- Recent surgery or illness
- Fatigue or strenuous activities during or shortly after the dive
- Dehydration
- Use of drugs or alcohol before or immediately after a dive
- Extremes in water temperature (cold dive or hot shower afterwards)
- Cramped position of arm or leg
- Pregnancy

Experts believe that divers get bent without knowing it because of their lack of knowledge of the bends, and the difficulty in recognizing the symptoms. You see, many of the symptoms can be attributed to something else (not getting enough sleep, sunburn, lifting diving equipment) especially when a diver has been "living it up" on vacation. According to DAN, dehydration is a proven risk factor in DCS. Alcohol directly causes dehydration by withdrawing body fluids when it is excreted in urine. The best method to avoid dehydration is to abstain from alcohol the night before a dive, during the dive day, and to drink plenty of non-alcoholic, caffeine-free fluids post dive. Remember, thirst is a sign that your body is already becoming dehydrated. Drink fluids continuously all day, even when you are not thirsty.

Symptoms usually appear between 15 minutes and 12 hours after surfacing, but in severe cases they may appear sooner. Ninety-eight percent of all symptoms usually appear in the first 24 hours. Delayed occurrence (over 24 hours) is rare, but can occur, especially if air travel follows diving.

Delaying or failing to seek treatment is probably one of the worst things the injured diver can do. Immediate treatment is most effective in preventing residual symptoms of the bends.

Decompression Sickness
Signs and Symptoms

— Tingling and itching of the skin

— Blotchy skin rash

— Local pain in arms, legs or joints

— Dizziness

— Loss of coordination

— Unusual fatigue or weakness

— Numbness or paralysis

— Shortness of breath/coughing spasms

— Collapse or unconsciousness

To minimize the risk of decompression sickness, always adhere to the Doppler limits. Do not make decompression dives, and be conservative when making multiday, multilevel, repetitive dives. Over half of the DCS victims reported to the DAN were performing either repetitive or multiday dives, and one third of all DCS victims were using a computer. An industry guideline also recommends that if you are multiday diving, you only make three dives per day and you skip a day of diving in the middle of the week. This guideline allows the body to off-gas any excess nitrogen that may have accumulated during consecutive days of diving.

Air Embolism

Another diving malady that can occur when scuba diving is an overexpansion problem. If a diver fails to exhale when ascending, the air trapped in the lungs will expand, rupturing the lungs and allowing air to escape into the bloodstream and body tissue. The worst place for an air embolism to occur is in the brain. The risk of a rapid or out-of-control ascent is increased when a diver must ascend from 100 or more feet (30+ metres), especially if the diver has poor buoyancy skills or panics. The signs and symptoms of an air embolism usually appear during or immediately after surfacing and may resemble those of a stroke.

Pneumothorax

Pneumothorax is another lung overexpansion problem. It occurs when air escapes into the space between the lung and the chest cavity and then expands, causing a lung collapse.

Mediastinal Emphysema

Mediastinal emphysema results when air becomes trapped in the cavity between the lungs and around the heart.

Air Embolism
Signs and Symptoms

— Dizziness
— Visual blurring and distortion
— Chest pain
— Personality change
— Paralysis or weakness
— Bloody froth from the mouth/nose
— Convulsions
— Unconsciousness
— Respiratory failure
— Loss of coordination

Pneumothorax
Signs and Symptoms

— Rapid, shallow breathing
— Sharp pain in chest
— Blue skin, lips and fingernails
— Rapid heartbeat

Mediastinal Emphysema
Signs and Symptoms

— Pain in chest, usually under breastbone
— Difficulty in breathing
— Faintness
— Change in voice

Subcutaneous Emphysema

Subcutaneous emphysema has the same cause as air embolism but the results are not as serious. Air escapes into the tissues underneath the skin, usually near the neck or collar bone.

The best way to avoid an overexpansion injury is to *never hold your breath.* In other words, breathe continuously. If you are not inhaling, exhale. This is especially important on ascent.

Subcutaneous Emphysema
Signs and Symptoms

— Difficulty in breathing & swallowing

— Change in sound of voice

— Swelling around face, neck and upper chest

— Crackling sensation when skin is touched

ACCIDENT MANAGEMENT

As a certified diver, you are not qualified to provide care to an accident victim unless you have had specialized training; however, you may be the first, or only, person at the scene so you should know how to take the appropriate steps for immediate care. Ideally, you should be trained to assess the accident situation, stabilize the victim through first aid and/or oxygen administration, and contact help immediately. It will be your job to relay the facts of the accident to the emergency medical personnel once they arrive.

If you are interested in learning more about accident management, you should enroll in an SSI *Diver Stress and Rescue* course and an SSI/NSC First Aid and CPR course at your local SSI Dealer. It is recommended that every diver be certified in CPR and First Aid, and it would also be advantageous to be trained in oxygen administration.

The current medical thinking describes both overexpansion injuries, including arterial gas embolism (AGE) and decompression sickness (DCS) as decompression illness (DCI) for purposes of treatment. These injuries have such similar symptoms that they should all be treated as decompression illness until such a time as it is determined otherwise. The injured diver will need immediate medical care, therefore getting proper medical help is your first priority.

Before transport to a medical facility, or until professional medical attention is available, the victim must be stabilized:

- Remove the injured person from danger.
- Manage the ABC's of basic life support.
- Provide 100% oxygen.
- Contact the local EMS (Emergency Medical Services) immediately.
- Call DAN at 1-919-684-8111.
- If the injury is serious, CPR or rescue breathing with the highest possible concentration of oxygen may be necessary.

Emergency Procedures and Contacts

Before you leave for your dive destination you should prepare a list of emergency procedures and numbers on a slate, or in your log book. You should know who to contact in the region where you will be diving in case of an emergency, and know the location of the nearest medical facility.

Included in your list should be the phone number of the nearest emergency medical service (EMS). DAN keeps a current list of all medical facilities on file throughout the world, so you can always contact them in an emergency.

Oxygen and Diving Accidents

One of the main responsibilities you will have as a first responder is to administer oxygen to the accident victim (Figure 4-3). Oxygen works in several ways to help the injured diver, and is probably the most important aspect of treatment, other than recompression. It can produce dramatic reversals in the diver's condition, even relieving severe symptoms such as paralysis.

According to DAN, administering oxygen to a conscious, spontaneously breathing person is not difficult and is considered the standard of care. Although the benefits of 100% oxygen have been proven, and it is difficult to further injure a diver with oxygen, it is recommended that the person administering oxygen be trained in the use of oxygen

Figure 4-3   *One of the main responsibilities you will have as a first responder is to administer oxygen to the accident victim.*

equipment and airway management. If your boat or dive group does not provide oxygen on site, you should know where to easily access it.

Check with your local SSI Authorized Dealer about courses in your local area. The Divers Alert Network (DAN) proves an excellent course in oxygen administration which is available through some SSI Dealers.

Emergency Medical Services (EMS)

The second step in the accident process is to contact emergency medical services (EMS) immediately. This may be a hospital, fire station, Coast Guard, water rescue team, or any other qualified personnel that are close to the accident site.

If you choose to transport the victim yourself, it is important that you go straight to an emergency medical facility such as a hospital. Do not go directly to a hyperbaric chamber. Most chambers are not staffed with doctors who can perform a medical evaluation, and besides, the victim may not require hyperbaric treatment as much as immediate medical treatment. In addition, contrary to what a lot of divers think, you cannot just go to a chamber facility and get treatment at any time (Figure 4-4). Authorities, whether government or private, set the guidelines for admission to these facilities, and some chambers require a doctor to authorize treatment. If you get heavily involved with deep diving after certification, you and your buddy, or local dive club, may want to visit a local chamber and learn what the protocol is for treatment. It is also interesting to learn about hyperbaric medicine and the recompression process.

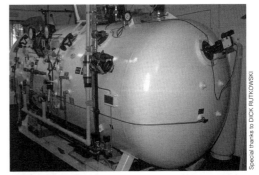

Special thanks to DICK RUTKOWSKI

Figure 4-4 *Contrary to what a lot of divers think, you cannot just go to a chamber facility and get treatment at any time.*

If deep dives are well planned and executed, there should be little chance of accident. However, since it is better to be safe than sorry, deep divers should understand the hazards of deep diving, the signs and symptoms of the diving maladies, especially decompression sickness, and be prepared with an emergency plan.

In Chapter 5 we will look at Repetitive Deep Diving and see how to make table and computer dives within the Doppler no-decompression limits.

CHAPTER 4
REVIEW

1. _____ _____ can cause dizziness or disorientation, and if the diver continues to descend, eventual unconsciousness.

2. The effects of _____ may be minimized by staying in good physical condition, eating a well-balanced diet, getting plenty of rest, and maintaining a _____ _____ schedule.

3. _____ _____ _____ is generally caused by unintentionally hyperventilating through shallow, rapid breathing while scuba diving.

4. When deep diving, DCS is usually caused by _____ _____ _____ at depth, or an improper ascent rate.

5. To minimize the risk of decompression sickness, always adhere to the _____ limits. Do not make decompression dives, and be conservative when making multiday, multilevel, _____ dives.

6. The signs and symptoms of an _____ _____ usually appear during or immediately after surfacing and may resemble those of a stroke.

7. _____ works in several ways to help the injured diver, and is probably the most important aspect of treatment, other than recompression.

8. The second step in the accident process is to contact _____ _____ _____ immediately.

REPETITIVE
DEEP DIVING
5

CHAPTER 5:
REPETITIVE
DEEP DIVING

For most divers it is just not enough to dive once and then call off the diving day, especially when you have traveled to an exotic diving resort or are diving from a live-aboard boat. Most divers like to make as many dives per day as they can. This is why diving computers have become so popular in recent years. They not only assist in dive planning, but they also allow you to increase your bottom time by giving credit for time spent at shallower depths. However, you do not have to use a computer. The dive tables are satisfactory for planning dives. To truly understand how to plan intelligent and responsible repetitive deep dives with the tables, let us go back and review the basics of nitrogen absorption and no-decompression diving.

REPETITIVE DIVING WITH THE DIVE TABLES

As we have already mentioned periodically throughout this manual, all deep dives should be planned within the Doppler no-decompression limits. We have also mentioned that Doppler ultrasound research indicates that all decreases in pressure cause the formation of "silent bubbles" in a diver from nitrogen coming out of solution. The U.S. Navy tables were based on the assumption that the bubbles will stay in solution as long as the partial pressure of nitrogen is not reduced by more than half. This research does not take into account the "silent bubbles," which is why the Doppler limits have been added to the SSI dive tables; the Navy limits have been removed to try and encourage divers to dive only within the Doppler limits. Anytime a diver pushes these limits there is an increased risk of decompression sickness.

Let us begin by reviewing how to plan a no-decompression repetitive dive with the tables. For our example we will say that our buddy team wants to plan their first dive to 120 feet (36 metres), and their second dive to 60 feet (18 metres). Let's look at how to plan the dive to see how much bottom time is available for each dive, as well as the required surface interval. You can refer to the dive tables in the appendix as needed.

Let's begin by looking at the maximum bottom time available for the first 120 foot dive, which is 10 minutes. If the team makes the dive for 10 minutes they will end the dive as a "D" diver. Now let's take a look at the surface interval. If they sit out somewhere between 1 hour 10 minutes and 2 hours 38 minutes, which is fairly realistic, they will end the surface interval as a "C" diver (Figure 5-1a).

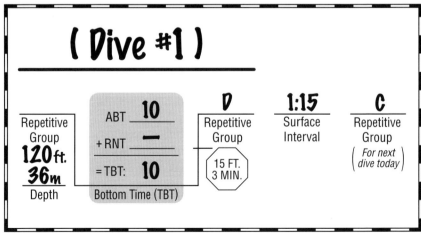

Figure 5-1a

Now let's look at our repetitive dive profile (Figure 5-1b) to see what bottom time is allowed for a second dive to 60 feet (18 metres). By looking at Table 3 you will see that the residual nitrogen time (RNT) for 60 feet is 17 minutes, and the adjusted no-decompression limit is 33 minutes. Thus if they plan for an actual bottom time (ABT) of 30 minutes and an RNT of 17 minutes they will end the dive with a total bottom time (TBT) of 47 minutes, which leaves them as "C" divers.

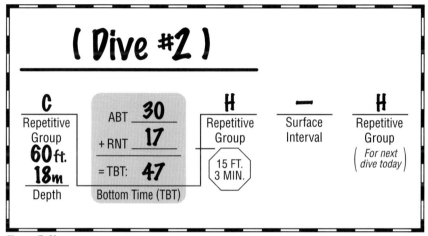

Figure 5-1b

You will see that a TBT of 47 minutes pushes the 60 foot (18 metre) no-decompression limit of 50 minutes. This allows little room for error. To be more conservative, the dive could be planned with a longer surface interval, with a shorter actual bottom time or to a shallower depth.

Omitted Decompression

Now that we have reviewed the Doppler limits, let us take a look at what divers should do if they accidentally exceed the Doppler no-decompression limits. In Chapter 1, Deep Dive Planning, we discussed how divers should make contingency dive plans for deeper depths, and how they should take the dive table slate under water in case the dive plan is exceeded. This will allow divers to quickly replan the dive and make sure the Doppler limits have not been exceeded. But what if they have been?

Decompression diving is defined as "a dive that exceeds the no-decompression limits of the U.S. Navy Dive Tables, thus requiring planned decompression stops to eliminate excess nitrogen accumulated during the dive." This type of diving is outside the industry standard for recreational diving. However, divers occasionally slip into an unplanned decompression situation as a result of staying too long at depth. When divers fail to stick to their no-decompression dive plan and exceed the dive table limits they need some way to get back to the surface and minimize the risk of decompression sickness. This is why we use an omitted decompression procedure (Figure 5-2).

Figure 5-2 *When divers fail to stick to their no-decompression dive plan, an omitted decompression procedure should be followed.*

Should you exceed the Doppler no-decompression time limits by less than 5 minutes on any dive, it is recommended that you ascend normally to 15 feet (5 metres) and stop for at least 10 minutes, or longer if your air supply allows. Should you exceed the Doppler no-decompression time limits by more than 5 minutes but less than 10 minutes on any dive, it is recommended that you stop at 15 feet (5 metres) for at least 20 minutes, or longer if your air supply allows. It is also recommended that you wait 24 hours to allow for off-gassing all of the excess nitrogen in your body before making another scuba dive. It would not be wise to "guess" at what your repetitive group designation would be so you could plan another dive. You do not know how much nitrogen you have actually absorbed or released. You can only approximate it through the tables, which are based on models and average absorption rates. If you have extended your bottom time beyond the limits of the tables you are already at increased risk for DCS. Diving again would only add to that risk.

As you can see, the diver's air supply becomes the limiting factor when performing an omitted decompression stop. This is, again, why it is recommended to have an additional air supply available at 15 feet (5 metres) on deep dives.

REPETITIVE DIVING WITH DIVE COMPUTERS

Dive computers are highly recommended for divers who intend to participate in repetitive, deep diving. Computers are designed to calculate your nitrogen absorption based on a theoretical model. They are considered by most diving experts to be more accurate for deep diving than the dive tables because they monitor your multi-level dive, giving you credit for all the time you spend at shallower depths. Most deep divers appreciate this because computers can increase your bottom time, which is a precious commodity to deep divers.

Most computer manufacturers do not recommend decompression diving with computers; however, they provide decompression stop information so your computer can assist you to the surface should you enter decompression mode (Figure 5-3). Refer to your manufacturer's directions for the special functions your computer provides.

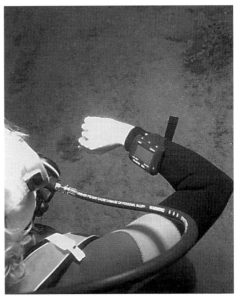

Figure 5-3 *Most computers provide decompression stop information to assist you to the surface should you enter decompression mode.*

Decompression Situation

If you are using a computer and not monitoring it, you run the risk of slipping into decompression mode. Your computer should be able to provide the decompression stop information needed to get to the surface. It will indicate at what depth you should make a decompression stop and for how long. Quality computers will also keep track of how much nitrogen you off-gas during any surface interval. This will be the most accurate reading of what "state" your body is in. When the computer says you have completely off-gassed, you can make another dive. However, should you not follow your computer, or if you omit a decompression stop, you should still adhere to the 24-hour waiting period before making another dive.

Be aware, however, that the computer is only as smart as it has been programmed to be. Certain decompression situations could make a computer shut down, or go into "violation" mode. This means that if your dive profile is outside the programming boundaries of your computer, it will not be able to make an accurate assessment of how to assist you to the surface, thus it may shut down. In this instance, you would be left to make a judgement on your ascent with no data to help you. Please read your manufacturer's directions on how to use your computer for decompression situations.

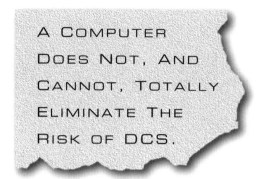

A COMPUTER DOES NOT, AND CANNOT, TOTALLY ELIMINATE THE RISK OF DCS.

A word of caution should be expressed that a computer does not, and cannot, totally eliminate the risk of DCS. No table or computer can guarantee your safety because of the many unknown and extenuating factors associated with DCS.

Computer Failure

Because your computer is an electronic, battery operated instrument it is possible that it could quit working while you are under water. While this may be unlikely, you should be prepared with back-up equipment and a back-up plan. Most manufacturers recommend the use of back-up instruments to help you ascend to the surface in the event of computer failure.

It is also recommended that you keep an accurate log of all of your dives during every surface interval. Thus, in theory, you would be able to complete your dive profile for that dive with your back-up instruments, then compute your group designation based on your last logged dive. However, if all of these pieces are not in place, it is recommended that you completely off-gas before making another scuba dive. Refer to the *AAUS Recommendations* in the Appendix for more detailed information, and refer to the owner's manual for your particular brand of dive computer.

Computer Training

It is recommended that computer users take a Specialty Course or orientation session prior to using their computers. You will learn general computer knowledge such as decompression theory and multi-level diving, and, more importantly, the specific information about your particular brand of computer such as its functions, the recommended way to dive with it, dealing with computer failure, and decompression situations. Talk to your SSI Dealer or Instructor to find out more about becoming a trained computer diver.

DECOMPRESSION DIVING

When a diver crosses the line and makes a decompression dive, a new realm of diving has been entered. The diver must fully understand the consequences and increased risk of decompression diving. This is not to say that some people do not perform decompression dives; however, this small group of divers is very experienced, with many logged dives. They also usually undergo extensive deep diving training, or learn through what could almost be considered an "apprenticeship" under the guidance of experienced deep divers. They are well planned, well equipped, well prepared and responsible—they understand and accept the consequences of what they are doing.

Decompression Diving Training

The recreational diving community does not advocate the practice of decompression diving, thus it is considered technical diving. Should you choose to participate in decompression diving it is highly recommended that you seek additional deep diving training, which is available from a variety of technical diving agencies that specialize in this type of technical diving training.

You can contact SSI or your local SSI Dealer to find out more about these technical diving training agencies.

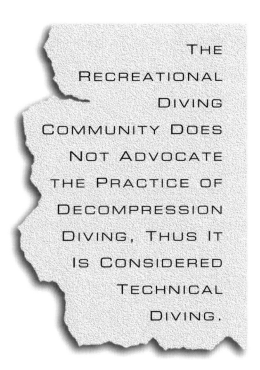

THE RECREATIONAL DIVING COMMUNITY DOES NOT ADVOCATE THE PRACTICE OF DECOMPRESSION DIVING, THUS IT IS CONSIDERED TECHNICAL DIVING.

SUMMARY

Deep diving can be an exciting and challenging adventure. Diving at greater depths opens up new wrecks, walls and other dive sites not available at shallower depths. It also provides a great sense of adventure to many divers, and satisfies our human curiosity that makes us wonder what lives in those dark waters below us.

However, responsible deep divers must also understand that they are putting themselves at increased risk to potential hazards and dive maladies such as decompression sickness. By planning properly and by using high quality scuba equipment and the necessary safety equipment, deep divers will lessen the chance of a problem and increase the chance of a successful dive!

Deep diving, even repetitive deep diving, can be executed with minimal risk. Deep dives can be planned well within the Doppler no-decompression limits, and bottom time can safely be added by learning to use a diving computer.

Remember, *Plan your Dive, and Dive your Plan!,* and you will be headed for a exciting deep diving adventure.

CHAPTER 5
REVIEW

1. The U.S. Navy tables were based on the assumption that the bubbles will stay in solution as long as the _____ _____ of nitrogen is not reduced by more than _____. This research does not take into account the " _____ _____ ," which is why the Doppler limits have been added to the SSI dive tables.

2. _____ diving is defined as "a dive that exceeds the no-decompression limits of the U.S. Navy Dive Tables."

3. Should you exceed the no-decompression time limits by less than 5 minutes on any dive, it is recommended that you ascend normally to 15 feet (5 metres) and stop for at least _____.

4. _____ _____ are highly recommended for divers who intend to participate in repetitive, deep diving.

5. It is recommended that computer users take a

_____   _____ or _____

_____ prior to using their computers.

6. The recreational diving community does not

advocate the practice of decompression diving, thus

it is considered _____

_____.

APPENDIX

APPENDIX 1

Tank Buoyancy And Specifications Charts

NOTE: *These charts contain general specifications. It is recommended that you contact the manufacturer of your tank for exact specifications*

Chart 1: Aluminum Tanks
COURTESY LUXFER USA LTD

CYLINDER CAPACITY (LBS.)	WEIGHT EMPTY (LBS.)	BUOYANCY FULL (LBS.)	BUOYANCY HALF FULL (LBS.)	BUOYANCY EMPTY (LBS.)
13.3	5.8	− 1.6	− 1.1	− 0.6
14.0	5.5	+ 0.6	+ 1.1	+ 1.6
30.0	11.9	− 1.1	0.0	+ 1.1
40.0	15.3	− 0.9	+ 0.6	+ 2.1
48.5	21.5	− 2.6	− 0.8	+ 1.0
63.0	26.9	− 2.3	0.0	+ 2.4
67.0	31.0	− 3.9	− 1.4	+ 1.2
69.6	28.5	− 1.7	+ 0.9	+ 3.5
74.0	30.3	− 1.7	+ 1.0	+ 3.8
77.4	31.7	− 1.8	+ 1.2	+ 4.1
80.0	35.2	− 3.3	− 0.3	+ 2.7
91.5	37.5	− 3.4	+ 0.3	+ 3.5
100.0	40.2	− 4.0	− 0.2	+ 3.5

Chart 2: Steel Tanks
COURTESY SCUBAPRO

CYLINDER CAPACITY (LBS.)	WEIGHT EMPTY (LBS.)	BUOYANCY FULL (LBS.)	BUOYANCY HALF FULL (LBS.)	BUOYANCY EMPTY (LBS.)
60.6	22.7	− 8.1	•	− 3.4
71.4	26.0	− 9.5	not	− 4.0
71.4	29.0	− 11.3	available	− 5.9
75.8	29.4	− 6.5		− 1.7
95.1	39.8	− 8.5	•	− 1.2

(−) = NEGATIVE BUOYANCY (the tank sinks)
(+) = POSITIVE BUOYANCY (the tank floats)

APPENDIX 2

Deep Dive Planning Sheet

Date: _____ Dive Site: _____

Your Name: _____ Qualified Depth: _____

Your Buddy's Name: _____ Qualified Depth: _____

Other Divers in Group: _____

Dive Objective: _____

☐ Review and recheck required equipment for all divers

☐ Surface support equipment:
  ☐ First Aid Kit
  ☐ Oxygen
  ☐ Spare System
  ☐ Descent/ascent lines
  ☐ Tie-Off System

☐ Self-evaluation and physical/ mental condition of all divers

☐ Review hand signals to be used

☐ Review entry method for dive site (safest and easiest)

☐ Review descent procedures and position of each team member

☐ Review dive abortion procedures

☐ Review ascent procedures

☐ Review exit method (safest and easiest)

☐ Review dive profile, maximum depth and bottom time

☐ Review estimated air required for each diver for planned depth

☐ Review minimum turnaround PSI/Bar (start up air)

☐ Review lost buddy procedure

☐ Review use of compass from area in case of separation of team

☐ Review emergency plan for surface handling of an emergency

APPENDIX 3

Metric Air Consumption Calculations

WC — Water Capacity: Measure of the internal volume of the cylinder.

WP — Working Pressure: Normal filling pressure of the cylinder.

WV — Working Volume: Amount of air the cylinder holds when filled to the working pressure. (WV = WC x WP in atms)

> Air Used $\dfrac{\text{Pressure Used x WV}}{\text{WP}}$
> (litres)

> For Example: (Starting Pressure) .....22 mpa
>   (Finish Pressure)........<u>10 mpa</u>
>   (Pressure Used) ....12 mpa

A 2500 litre cylinder has a **WP** of 22.4 mpa and a **WV** of approximately 2500 litres.

$$\left(\frac{12\ mpa}{22.4\ mpa} \right)\ x\ 2500\ litres\ =\ 1339\ litres$$

SM — Surface Minutes: The number of minutes at a particular depth multiplied by the absolute pressure in atmospheres.

> For Example: A dive to 4 atmospheres (30 metres) for 25 minutes equals 100 **SM.**

$$25\ minutes\ x\ 4\ atms\ =\ 100\ \textbf{SM}$$

SCR — Surface Consumption Rate: Amount of air consumed in litres per minutes. The amount is figured by dividing SM into the number of litres used.

$$\frac{1339\ litres\ (air\ used)}{100\ minutes\ (SM)}\ =\ SCR\ of\ 13.4\ litres\ per\ minute$$

Air Required for Dive = *SM x SCR*

The required air must not exceed 80% of the cylinder's WC, including the air required for the ascent and safety stop. A 20% safety margin is left for contingencies or emergencies.

APPENDIX 4

AAUS Recommendations

The AAUS has held workshops dealing with diving safety and dive computer use. The following recommendations for general diving practices were compiled from three of its workshops. We would like to thank Karl Huggins for compiling this information, and the AAUS for allowing us to reprint it here.

- Each diver relying on a dive computer to plan dives and indicate or determine decompression status must have their own unit.
- On any given dive, both divers in the buddy pair must follow the most conservative dive computer.
- If the dive computer fails at any time during the dive, the dive must be terminated and appropriate surfacing procedures should be initiated immediately.
- A diver should not dive for 24 hours before activating a dive computer to use it to control his or her diving.
- Once a dive computer is in use, it must **not** be switched off until it indicates complete outgassing has occurred, 24 hours have elapsed (whichever comes first), or if no more dives are planned over the next few days.
- When using a dive computer, non-emergency ascents are to be at the rate(s) specified for the table, or make and model of dive computer being used.
- Ascent rates shall not excess 30 feet per minute (9 metres per minute).
- A safety stop in the 10 to 30 foot zone (3 to 9 metres) for 3 to 5 minutes is recommended on every dive.
- Repetitive and multi-level diving procedures should start the dive, or the series of dives, at the maximum planned depth, followed by subsequent dives of shallower exposures.[5]
- Multiple deep dives should be avoided.
- Breathing 100% oxygen above water is preferred to in-water air procedures for omitted decompression.[5]
- It is recommended that attention of divers be directed with emphasis on the ancillary factors to decompression risk such as fitness to dive, adequate rest, hydration, body weight, age, and especially rate of ascent which should not be more than 30 feet per minute (9 metres).[7]
- Divers are encouraged to learn and remember the signs and symptoms of decompression illness and report them promptly so as to receive effective treatment as rapidly as possible to prevent residual injury.[7]
- The use of oxygen breathing on the surface, whenever possible via a demand regulator mask system, to ensure the highest percentage of oxygen to the patient, is recommended while awaiting treatment if decompression illness is thought to be present. The use of 100% oxygen in the water while awaiting treatment is not recommended for recreational diving.

5. Lang, M. and Hamilton, R., *Proceedings of the American Academy of Underwater Sciences Dive Computer Workshop*, (University of Southern California Sea Grant Program, 1989.)

6. Lang, M. and Egstrom, G., *Proceedings of the American Academy of Underwater Sciences Biomechanics of Safe Ascents Workshop*, (Costa Mesa: American Academy of Underwater Sciences, 1990).

7. Lang, M. and Vann, R., *Proceedings of the American Academy of Underwater Sciences Repetitive Diving Workshop*, (Costa Mesa: American Academy of Underwater Sciences, 1992).

APPENDIX 5a

SSI Dive Tables

DOPPLER NO-DECOMPRESSION LIMITS BASED ON U.S. NAVY DIVE TABLES

SCUBA SCHOOLS INTERNATIONAL **SSI**®

TABLE 1 No-Decompression Limits and Repetitive Group Designation Table For No-Decompression Air Dives

HOW TO USE TABLE 1: Find the planned depth of your dive in feet or metres at the far left of Table 1. Read to the right until you find the time (minutes) you plan to spend at that depth. Read down to find the Group Designation letter.

DEPTH feet / metres		Doppler No-Decompression Limits (minutes)											
10	3.0		60	120	210	300							
15	4.5		35	70	110	160	225	350					
20	6.0		25	50	75	100	135	180	240	325			
25	7.5	245	20	35	55	75	100	125	160	195	245		
30	9.0	205	15	30	45	60	75	95	120	145	170	205	
35	10.5	160	5	15	25	40	50	60	80	100	120	140	160
40	12.0	130	5	15	25	30	40	50	70	80	100	110	130
50	15.0	70		10	15	25	30	40	50	60	70		
60	18.0	50		10	15	20	25	30	40	50			
70	21.0	40		5	10	15	20	30	35	40			
80	24.0	30		5	10	15	20	25	30				
90	27.0	25		5	10	12	15	20	25				
100	30.0	20		5	7	10	15	20					
110	33.0	15			5	10	13	15					
120	36.0	10			5	10							
130	39.0	5			5								

GROUP DESIGNATION: **A B C D E F G H I J K**

HOW TO USE TABLE 2:

Enter with the Group Designation letter from Table 1. Follow the arrow down to the corresponding letter on Table 2. To the left of these letters are windows of time. Read to the left until you find the times between which your surface interval falls. Then read down until you find your New Group Designation letter. Dives following surface intervals of more than 12 hours are not repetitive dives.

TABLE 2 Residual Nitrogen Timetable For Repetitive Air Dives

REPETITIVE GROUP AT THE BEGINNING OF THE SURFACE INTERVAL

0:10 12:00*	**A**									
3:21 12:00*	0:10 3:20	**B**								
4:50 12:00*	1:40 4:49	0:10 1:39	**C**							
5:49 12:00*	2:39 5:48	1:10 2:38	0:10 1:09	**D**						
6:35 12:00*	3:25 6:34	1:58 3:24	0:55 1:57	0:10 0:54	**E**					
7:06 12:00*	3:58 7:05	2:29 3:57	1:30 2:28	0:46 1:29	0:10 0:45	**F**				
7:36 12:00*	4:26 7:35	2:59 4:25	2:00 2:58	1:16 1:59	0:41 1:15	0:10 0:40	**G**			
8:00 12:00*	4:50 7:59	3:21 4:49	2:24 3:20	1:42 2:23	1:07 1:41	0:37 1:06	0:10 0:36	**H**		
8:22 12:00*	5:13 8:21	3:44 5:12	2:45 3:43	2:03 2:44	1:30 2:02	1:00 1:29	0:34 0:59	0:10 0:33	**I**	
8:51 12:00*	5:41 8:50	4:03 5:40	3:05 4:02	2:21 3:04	1:48 2:20	1:20 1:47	0:55 1:19	0:32 0:54	0:10 0:31	**J**
8:59 12:00*	5:49 8:58	4:20 5:48	3:22 4:19	2:39 3:21	2:04 2:38	1:36 2:03	1:12 1:35	0:50 1:11	0:29 0:49	0:10 0:28	**K**

NEW GROUP DESIGNATION ▶	**A**	**B**	**C**	**D**	**E**	**F**	**G**	**H**	**I**	**J**	**K**
REPETITIVE DIVE DEPTH ▼	▼RESIDUAL NITROGEN TIMES DISPLAYED ON REVERSE▼										

© 1995 CONCEPT SYSTEMS. INC.

Reorder Nº 2206